MW00395807

The Cast of Characters as recorded in the Old Testament

A Guide for Bible Study

Compiled by
Rita Kleve

CrossHouse

Published by
CrossHouse Publishing
PO Box 461592
Garland, Texas 75046-1592

Printed in the United States of America
by Lightning Source, LaVergne, TN
Cover design by Dennis Davidson

ISBN 978-1-934749-32-6

Library of Congress Control Number 2008935579

In Dedication

To God, the Father

To my husband, Gene Kleve,
and to our children
Jonathan Kleve
Matthew Kleve
Mitchell Kleve
and their families

To Reverend Gary Rahe

To Reverend Neal Pfister

and

To the memory of my loving parents,
Conrad and Mary Brunken

Introduction

A friend once told me that the Bible is the road map to life. I believe that to be most certainly true. It is a guidebook to be read and headed. However, some who read it might find that the seemingly endless names mentioned in the Old Testament are boring, confusing, and unnecessary. Yet, one cannot read a good novel without a cast of exciting characters.

Using a family tree format, this book includes all the persons with family connections as recorded in the Old Testament. Of course, there are those persons and families mentioned whose family connection cannot be identified. Certain tribes were more predominate than others. With more than thirteen hundred individuals and more than twelve hundred families, it is an extensive family tree. Each entry of the tree notes the Old Testament book, chapter and verse where that person is first mentioned. Many additional informational notations are included throughout the study as well with room for the reader's own notations. Read the Old Testament while using this *Cast of Characters* as your reference. It will make Bible study more interesting and easier to understand.

Who are all these people in the Old Testament? First and foremost, this is God's "chosen family." It is the family that would one day include His son, Jesus. They are an imperfect family with strengths and weaknesses, goodness and evil, those rich and those poor. There were persons who loved the Lord and the ones who did not. Even those who loved the Lord continued to struggle with sin. They are a *Cast of Characters.*

It is a family not so different from families in today's world. From the time of Adam until today, we have all sinned. No matter how hard we try to do God's will, we fail. The good news is that God loves us anyway and always will. He loves us so much that He sent His son, Jesus, into the world to die so that we might live.

Contents

Adam to Noah 1-2

Noah to Isaac 3-6

Isaac and Rebekah. 7

Esau 8

Tribes of Gad and Asher 9-11

Tribes of Dan and Naphtali. 12

Tribes of Manasseh and Ephraim 13-14

Tribe of Benjamin 15-21

Tribes of Reuben and Zebulun 22

Tribe of Issachar 23-24

Tribe of Simeon 25-26

Tribe of Levi 27-34

Tribe of Judah 35-46

Summary of the Kings of Israel 47

Index of Characters. 48-54

Reference Charts 55-62

Resources 63

And the Lord God formed man
from the dust of the ground and
breathed into his nostrils the breath
of life, and man became a living being.
Genesis 2:7

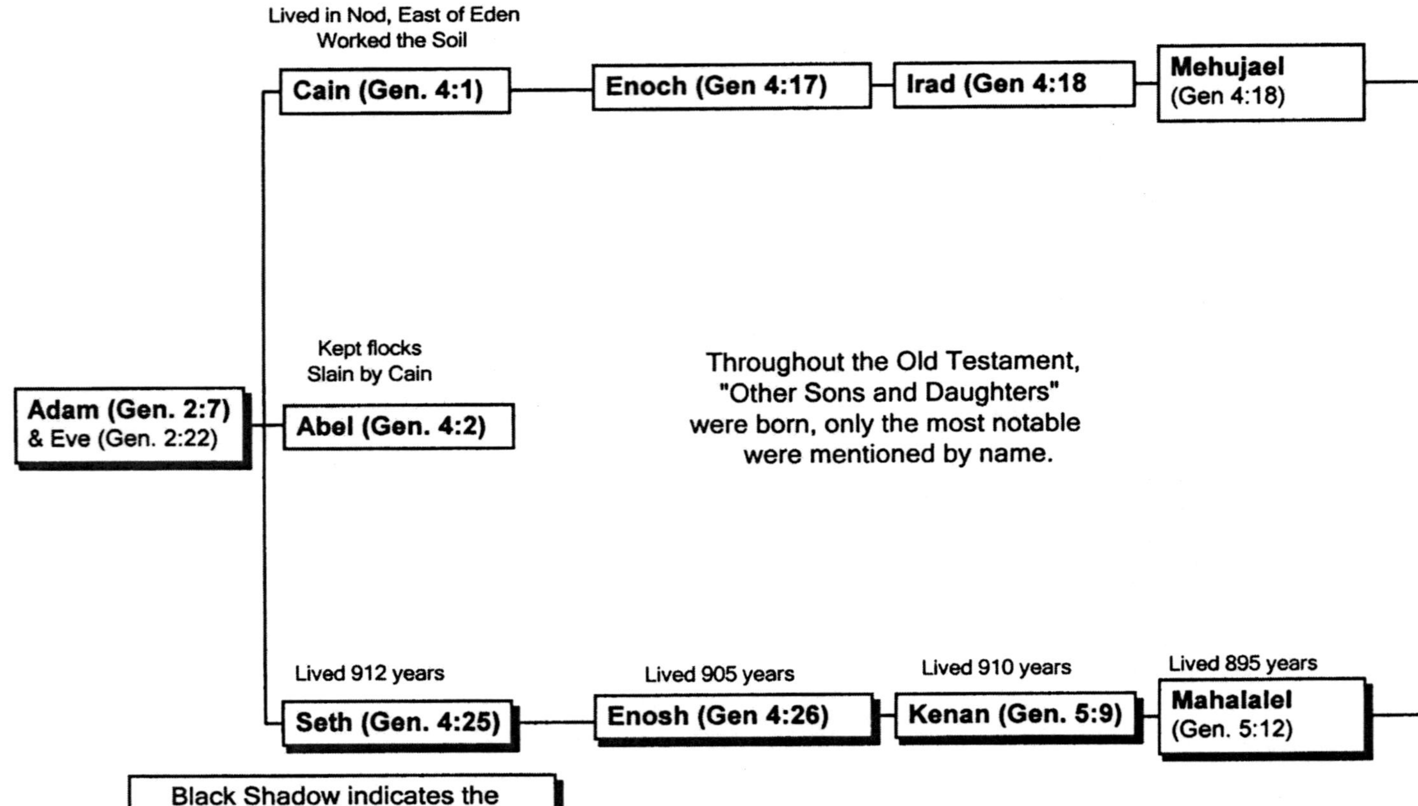
Lived in Nod, East of Eden
Worked the Soil
Cain (Gen. 4:1)
Enoch (Gen 4:17)
Irad (Gen 4:18
Mehujael (Gen 4:18)
Kept flocks
Slain by Cain
Adam (Gen. 2:7) & Eve (Gen. 2:22)
Abel (Gen. 4:2)
Throughout the Old Testament, "Other Sons and Daughters" were born, only the most notable were mentioned by name.
Lived 912 years
Seth (Gen. 4:25)
Lived 905 years
Enosh (Gen 4:26)
Lived 910 years
Kenan (Gen. 5:9)
Lived 895 years
Mahalalel (Gen. 5:12)

Black Shadow indicates the Genealogy of Jesus

as recorded in the lineage of Joseph Matthew 1:1-17

Why Joseph and not MARY?

In those days, Genealogy Records were kept in more detail for men than for women. However, as was the practice, women were to marry someone within her fathers' tribe.

Every daughter....must marry someone in her father's tribalclan.... (Deuteronomy 36:8)

Some Bible Scholars believe that the lineage of Mary is recorded in Luke 3:23:28

Other Bible Scholars consider that Matthew gives the lineage of Mary and Luke gives lineage of Joseph.

When the two genealogies are compared, it is evident that both Mary and Joseph were descended from King David thereby establishing His title to the throne. See pages 41-42.

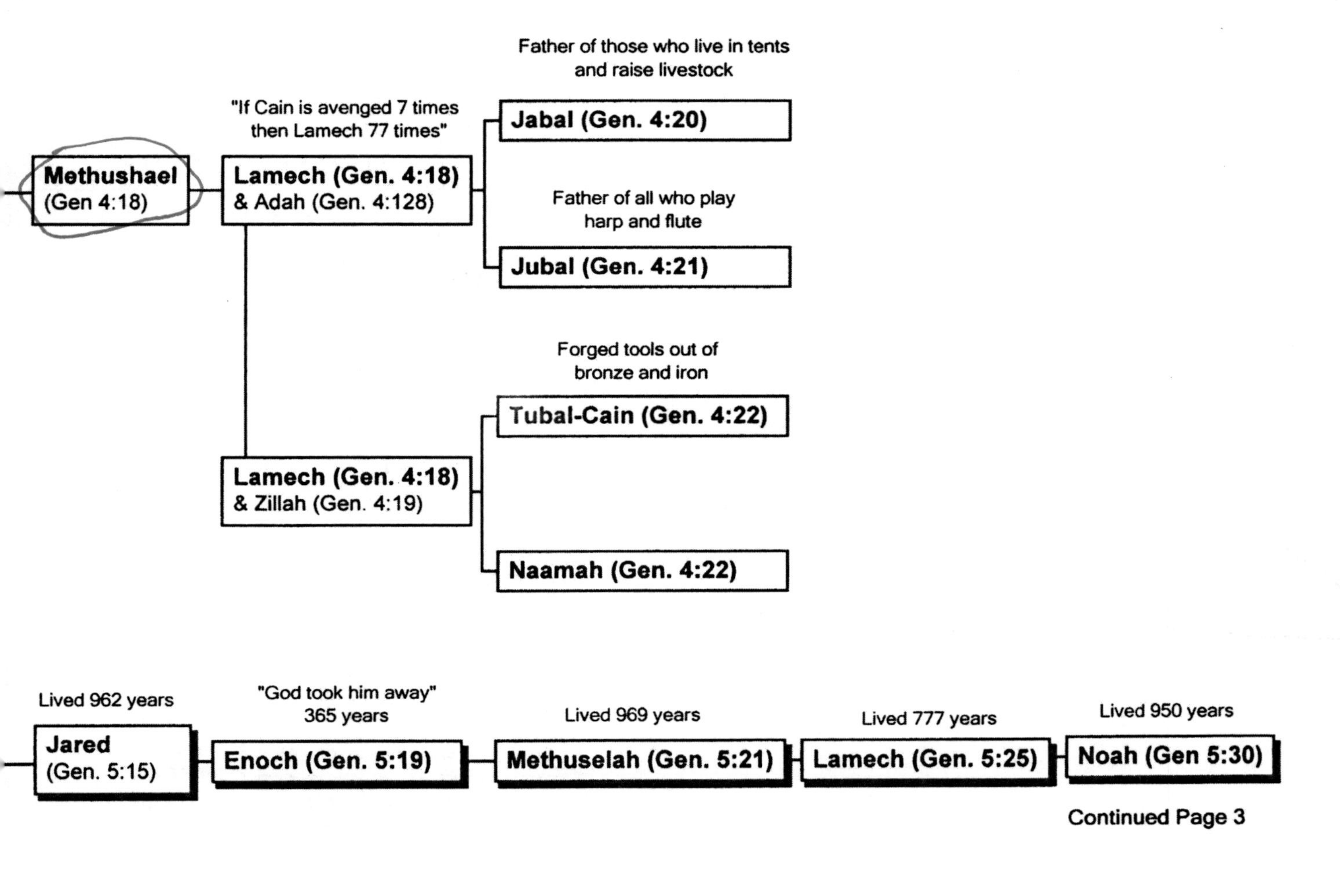
Father of those who live in tents
and raise livestock
"If Cain is avenged 7 times
then Lamech 77 times"
Jabal (Gen. 4:20)
Methushael
(Gen 4:18)
Lamech (Gen. 4:18)
& Adah (Gen. 4:128)
Father of all who play
harp and flute
Jubal (Gen. 4:21)
Forged tools out of
bronze and iron
Tubal-Cain (Gen. 4:22)
Lamech (Gen. 4:18)
& Zillah (Gen. 4:19)
Naamah (Gen. 4:22)
Lived 962 years
Jared
(Gen. 5:15)
"God took him away"
365 years
Enoch (Gen. 5:19)
Lived 969 years
Methuselah (Gen. 5:21)
Lived 777 years
Lamech (Gen. 5:25)
Lived 950 years
Noah (Gen 5:30)
Continued Page 3

And then the Lord said, "My Spirit will not contend with man forever, for he is mortal; his days will be a hundred and twenty years."
Genesis 6:3

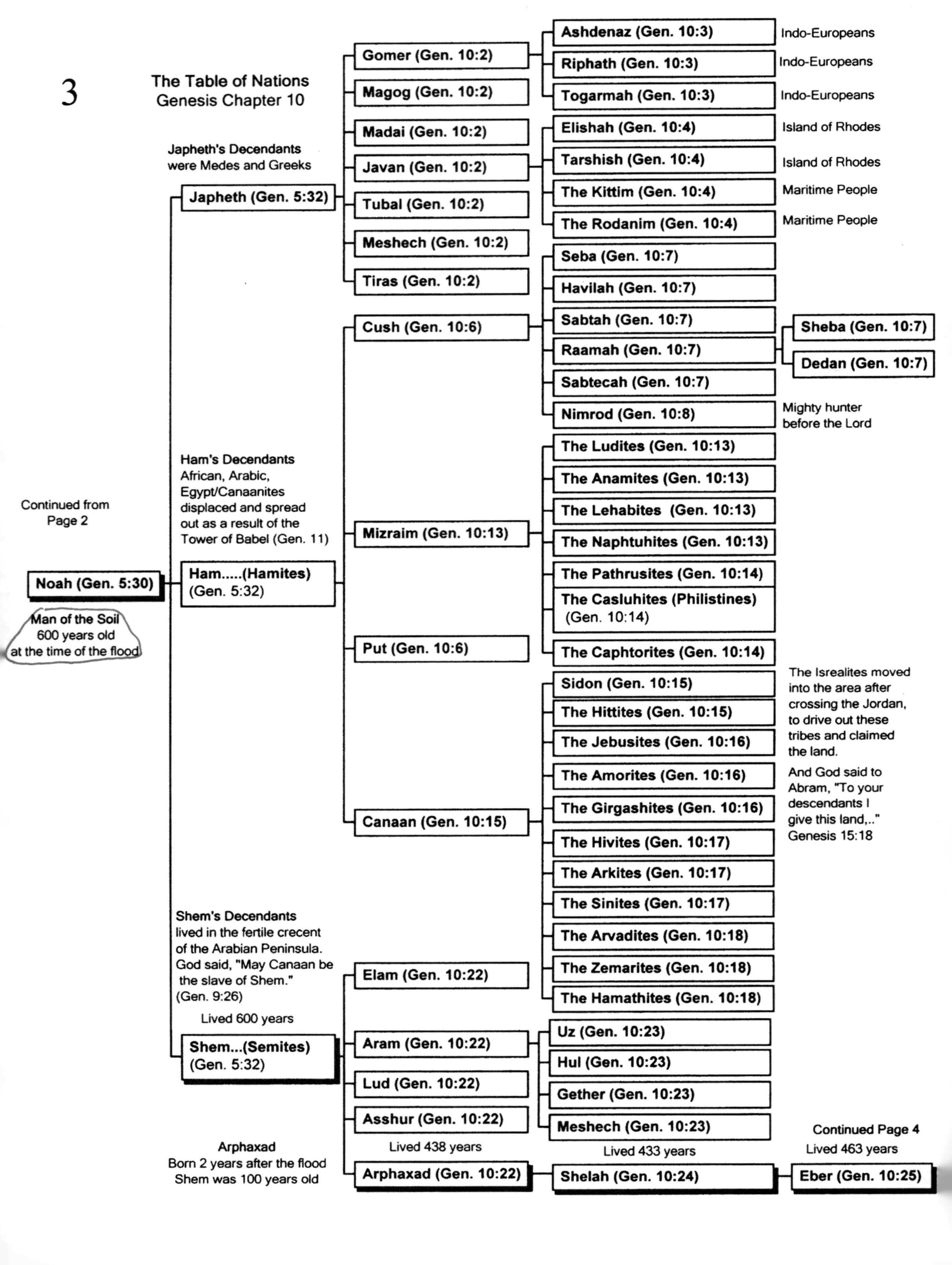
The Table of Nations
Genesis Chapter 10
Japheth's Decendants
were Medes and Greeks
Japheth (Gen. 5:32)
Gomer (Gen. 10:2)
Magog (Gen. 10:2)
Madai (Gen. 10:2)
Javan (Gen. 10:2)
Tubal (Gen. 10:2)
Meshech (Gen. 10:2)
Tiras (Gen. 10:2)
Ashdenaz (Gen. 10:3)
Indo-Europeans
Riphath (Gen. 10:3)
Indo-Europeans
Togarmah (Gen. 10:3)
Indo-Europeans
Elishah (Gen. 10:4)
Island of Rhodes
Tarshish (Gen. 10:4)
Island of Rhodes
The Kittim (Gen. 10:4)
Maritime People
The Rodanim (Gen. 10:4)
Maritime People
Cush (Gen. 10:6)
Seba (Gen. 10:7)
Havilah (Gen. 10:7)
Sabtah (Gen. 10:7)
Raamah (Gen. 10:7)
Sheba (Gen. 10:7)
Dedan (Gen. 10:7)
Sabtecah (Gen. 10:7)
Nimrod (Gen. 10:8)
Mighty hunter
before the Lord
Ham's Decendants
African, Arabic,
Egypt/Canaanites
displaced and spread
out as a result of the
Tower of Babel (Gen. 11)
Continued from
Page 2
Noah (Gen. 5:30)
Man of the Soil
600 years old
at the time of the flood
Ham.....(Hamites)
(Gen. 5:32)
Mizraim (Gen. 10:13)
The Ludites (Gen. 10:13)
The Anamites (Gen. 10:13)
The Lehabites (Gen. 10:13)
The Naphtuhites (Gen. 10:13)
The Pathrusites (Gen. 10:14)
The Casluhites (Philistines)
(Gen. 10:14)
The Caphtorites (Gen. 10:14)
Put (Gen. 10:6)
Canaan (Gen. 10:15)
Sidon (Gen. 10:15)
The Hittites (Gen. 10:15)
The Jebusites (Gen. 10:16)
The Amorites (Gen. 10:16)
The Girgashites (Gen. 10:16)
The Hivites (Gen. 10:17)
The Arkites (Gen. 10:17)
The Sinites (Gen. 10:17)
The Arvadites (Gen. 10:18)
The Zemarites (Gen. 10:18)
The Hamathites (Gen. 10:18)
The Isrealites moved
into the area after
crossing the Jordan,
to drive out these
tribes and claimed
the land.
And God said to
Abram, "To your
descendants I
give this land,.."
Genesis 15:18
Shem's Decendants
lived in the fertile crecent
of the Arabian Peninsula.
God said, "May Canaan be
the slave of Shem."
(Gen. 9:26)
Lived 600 years
Shem...(Semites)
(Gen. 5:32)
Elam (Gen. 10:22)
Aram (Gen. 10:22)
Lud (Gen. 10:22)
Asshur (Gen. 10:22)
Uz (Gen. 10:23)
Hul (Gen. 10:23)
Gether (Gen. 10:23)
Meshech (Gen. 10:23)
Arphaxad
Born 2 years after the flood
Shem was 100 years old
Lived 438 years
Arphaxad (Gen. 10:22)
Lived 433 years
Shelah (Gen. 10:24)
Continued Page 4
Lived 463 years
Eber (Gen. 10:25)

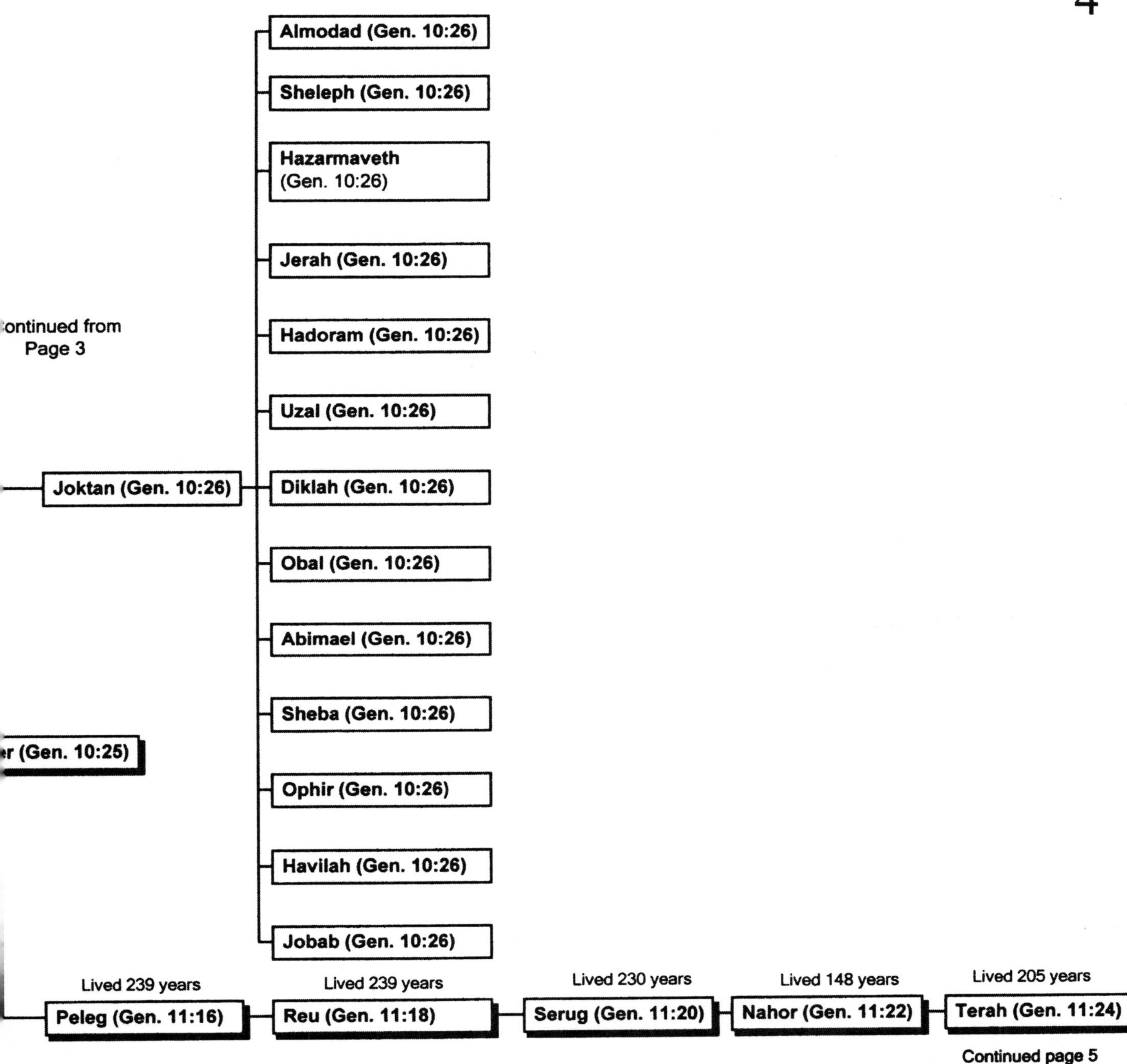

Almodad (Gen. 10:26)
Sheleph (Gen. 10:26)
Hazarmaveth (Gen. 10:26)
Jerah (Gen. 10:26)
ontinued from Page 3
Hadoram (Gen. 10:26)
Uzal (Gen. 10:26)
Joktan (Gen. 10:26)
Diklah (Gen. 10:26)
Obal (Gen. 10:26)
Abimael (Gen. 10:26)
Sheba (Gen. 10:26)
r (Gen. 10:25)
Ophir (Gen. 10:26)
Havilah (Gen. 10:26)
Jobab (Gen. 10:26)
Lived 239 years
Peleg (Gen. 11:16)
Lived 239 years
Reu (Gen. 11:18)
Lived 230 years
Serug (Gen. 11:20)
Lived 148 years
Nahor (Gen. 11:22)
Lived 205 years
Terah (Gen. 11:24)
Continued page 5

The reason for his being named Peleg,
is that "in his time the earth was divided".
This probably refers to the confounding of the language
and the consequent scattering of the decendents of Noah.

Genesis 11:1-9

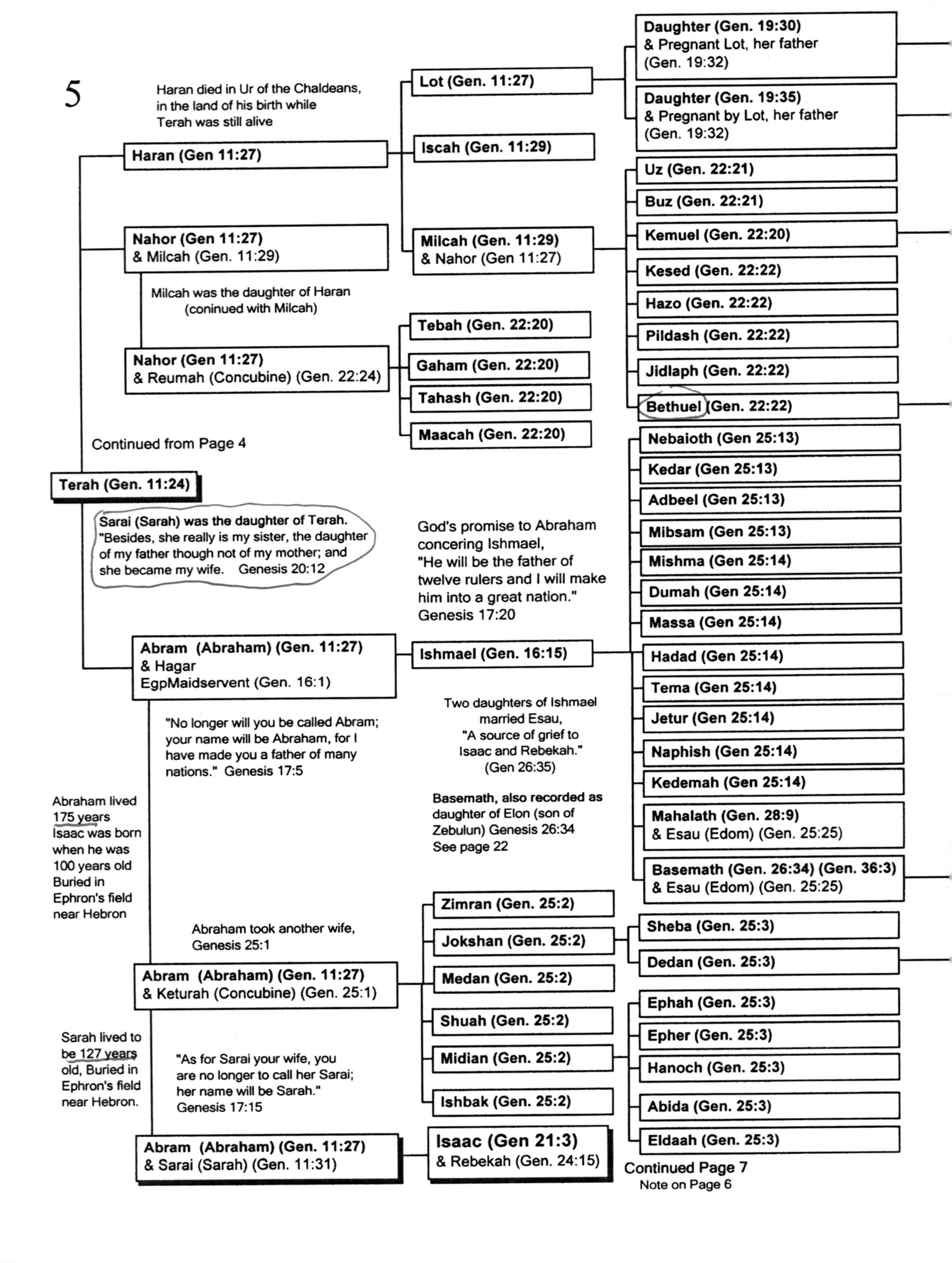

5
Haran died in Ur of the Chaldeans, in the land of his birth while Terah was still alive
Daughter (Gen. 19:30) & Pregnant Lot, her father (Gen. 19:32)
Lot (Gen. 11:27)
Daughter (Gen. 19:35) & Pregnant by Lot, her father (Gen. 19:32)
Haran (Gen 11:27)
Iscah (Gen. 11:29)
Uz (Gen. 22:21)
Buz (Gen. 22:21)
Nahor (Gen 11:27) & Milcah (Gen. 11:29)
Milcah (Gen. 11:29) & Nahor (Gen 11:27)
Kemuel (Gen. 22:20)
Kesed (Gen. 22:22)
Milcah was the daughter of Haran (coninued with Milcah)
Hazo (Gen. 22:22)
Tebah (Gen. 22:20)
Pildash (Gen. 22:22)
Nahor (Gen 11:27) & Reumah (Concubine) (Gen. 22:24)
Gaham (Gen. 22:20)
Jidlaph (Gen. 22:22)
Tahash (Gen. 22:20)
Bethuel (Gen. 22:22)
Maacah (Gen. 22:20)
Continued from Page 4
Nebaioth (Gen 25:13)
Kedar (Gen 25:13)
Terah (Gen. 11:24)
Adbeel (Gen 25:13)
Sarai (Sarah) was the daughter of Terah. "Besides, she really is my sister, the daughter of my father though not of my mother; and she became my wife. Genesis 20:12
God's promise to Abraham concering Ishmael, "He will be the father of twelve rulers and I will make him into a great nation." Genesis 17:20
Mibsam (Gen 25:13)
Mishma (Gen 25:14)
Dumah (Gen 25:14)
Massa (Gen 25:14)
Abram (Abraham) (Gen. 11:27) & Hagar EgpMaidservent (Gen. 16:1)
Ishmael (Gen. 16:15)
Hadad (Gen 25:14)
Tema (Gen 25:14)
Two daughters of Ishmael married Esau, "A source of grief to Isaac and Rebekah." (Gen 26:35)
Jetur (Gen 25:14)
"No longer will you be called Abram; your name will be Abraham, for I have made you a father of many nations." Genesis 17:5
Naphish (Gen 25:14)
Kedemah (Gen 25:14)
Abraham lived 175 years Isaac was born when he was 100 years old Buried in Ephron's field near Hebron
Basemath, also recorded as daughter of Elon (son of Zebulun) Genesis 26:34 See page 22
Mahalath (Gen. 28:9) & Esau (Edom) (Gen. 25:25)
Basemath (Gen. 26:34) (Gen. 36:3) & Esau (Edom) (Gen. 25:25)
Zimran (Gen. 25:2)
Sheba (Gen. 25:3)
Abraham took another wife, Genesis 25:1
Jokshan (Gen. 25:2)
Dedan (Gen. 25:3)
Abram (Abraham) (Gen. 11:27) & Keturah (Concubine) (Gen. 25:1)
Medan (Gen. 25:2)
Ephah (Gen. 25:3)
Shuah (Gen. 25:2)
Epher (Gen. 25:3)
Sarah lived to be 127 years old, Buried in Ephron's field near Hebron.
"As for Sarai your wife, you are no longer to call her Sarai; her name will be Sarah." Genesis 17:15
Midian (Gen. 25:2)
Hanoch (Gen. 25:3)
Ishbak (Gen. 25:2)
Abida (Gen. 25:3)
Eldaah (Gen. 25:3)
Abram (Abraham) (Gen. 11:27) & Sarai (Sarah) (Gen. 11:31)
Isaac (Gen 21:3) & Rebekah (Gen. 24:15)
Continued Page 7
Note on Page 6

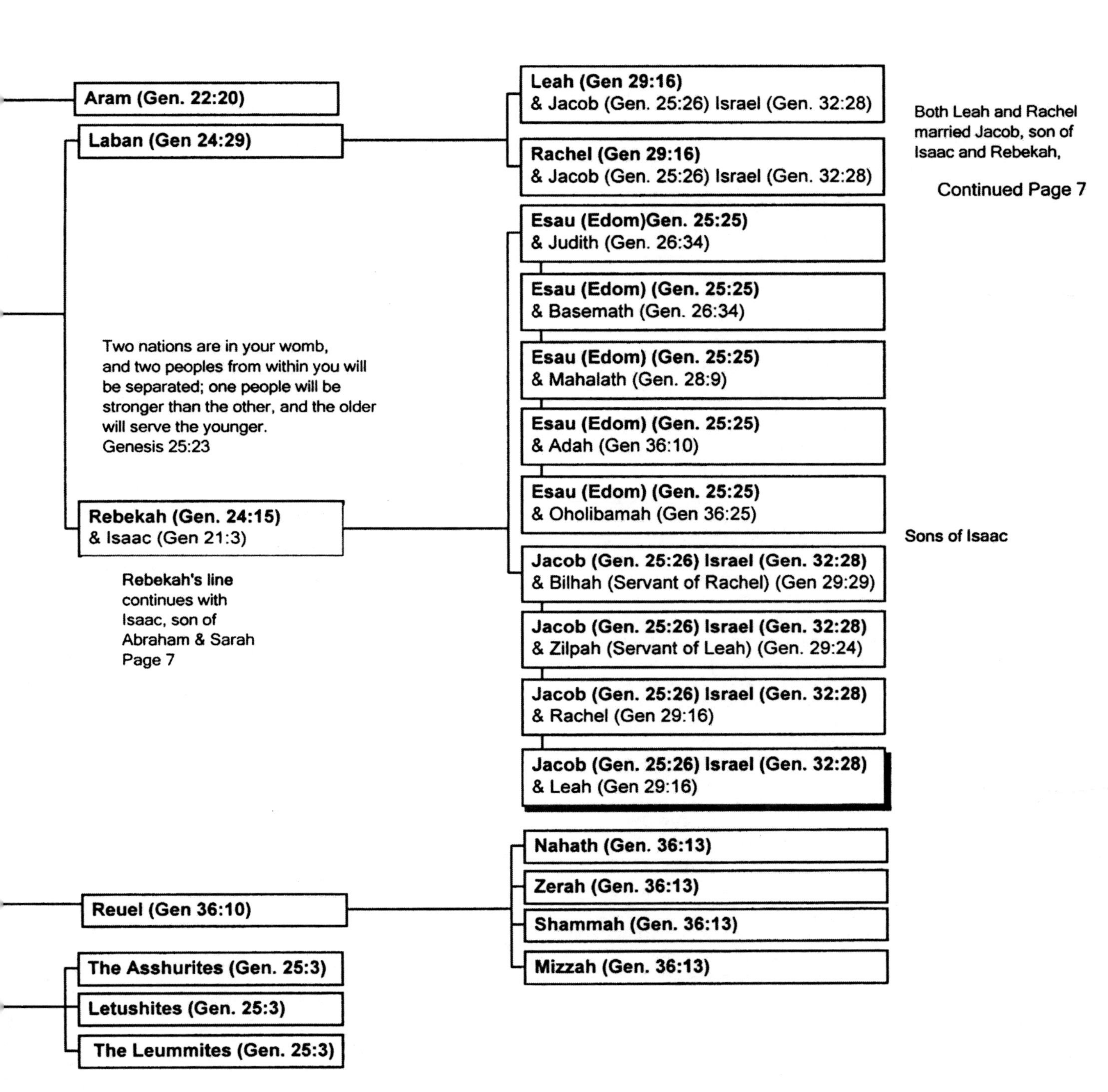
Moab (Gen. 19:37)
Moabites
Ben-Ammi (Gen. 19:38)
Ammonites
Aram (Gen. 22:20)
Laban (Gen 24:29)
Leah (Gen 29:16)
& Jacob (Gen. 25:26) Israel (Gen. 32:28)
Rachel (Gen 29:16)
& Jacob (Gen. 25:26) Israel (Gen. 32:28)
Both Leah and Rachel married Jacob, son of Isaac and Rebekah,
Continued Page 7
Esau (Edom)Gen. 25:25)
& Judith (Gen. 26:34)
Esau (Edom) (Gen. 25:25)
& Basemath (Gen. 26:34)
Esau (Edom) (Gen. 25:25)
& Mahalath (Gen. 28:9)
Esau (Edom) (Gen. 25:25)
& Adah (Gen 36:10)
Esau (Edom) (Gen. 25:25)
& Oholibamah (Gen 36:25)
Two nations are in your womb, and two peoples from within you will be separated; one people will be stronger than the other, and the older will serve the younger.
Genesis 25:23
Rebekah (Gen. 24:15)
& Isaac (Gen 21:3)
Sons of Isaac
Jacob (Gen. 25:26) Israel (Gen. 32:28)
& Bilhah (Servant of Rachel) (Gen 29:29)
Rebekah's line continues with Isaac, son of Abraham & Sarah Page 7
Jacob (Gen. 25:26) Israel (Gen. 32:28)
& Zilpah (Servant of Leah) (Gen. 29:24)
Jacob (Gen. 25:26) Israel (Gen. 32:28)
& Rachel (Gen 29:16)
Jacob (Gen. 25:26) Israel (Gen. 32:28)
& Leah (Gen 29:16)
Nahath (Gen. 36:13)
Zerah (Gen. 36:13)
Reuel (Gen 36:10)
Shammah (Gen. 36:13)
Mizzah (Gen. 36:13)
The Asshurites (Gen. 25:3)
Letushites (Gen. 25:3)
The Leummites (Gen. 25:3)

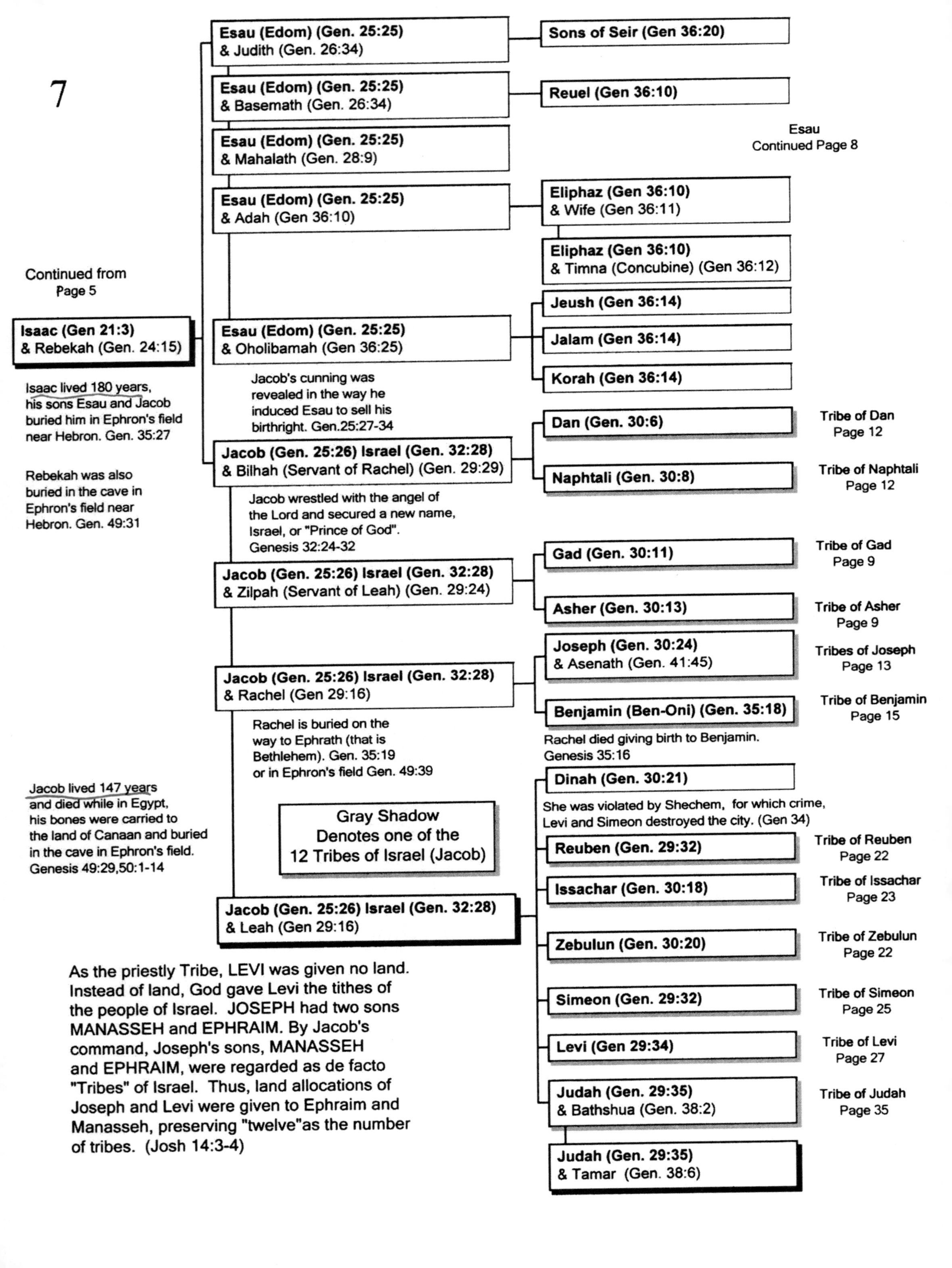
7
Continued from
Page 5
Isaac (Gen 21:3)
& Rebekah (Gen. 24:15)
Isaac lived 180 years, his sons Esau and Jacob buried him in Ephron's field near Hebron. Gen. 35:27
Rebekah was also buried in the cave in Ephron's field near Hebron. Gen. 49:31
Esau (Edom) (Gen. 25:25)
& Judith (Gen. 26:34)
Sons of Seir (Gen 36:20)
Esau (Edom) (Gen. 25:25)
& Basemath (Gen. 26:34)
Reuel (Gen 36:10)
Esau (Edom) (Gen. 25:25)
& Mahalath (Gen. 28:9)
Esau
Continued Page 8
Esau (Edom) (Gen. 25:25)
& Adah (Gen 36:10)
Eliphaz (Gen 36:10)
& Wife (Gen 36:11)
Eliphaz (Gen 36:10)
& Timna (Concubine) (Gen 36:12)
Esau (Edom) (Gen. 25:25)
& Oholibamah (Gen 36:25)
Jeush (Gen 36:14)
Jalam (Gen 36:14)
Korah (Gen 36:14)
Jacob's cunning was revealed in the way he induced Esau to sell his birthright. Gen.25:27-34
Jacob (Gen. 25:26) Israel (Gen. 32:28)
& Bilhah (Servant of Rachel) (Gen. 29:29)
Dan (Gen. 30:6)
Tribe of Dan
Page 12
Naphtali (Gen. 30:8)
Tribe of Naphtali
Page 12
Jacob wrestled with the angel of the Lord and secured a new name, Israel, or "Prince of God". Genesis 32:24-32
Jacob (Gen. 25:26) Israel (Gen. 32:28)
& Zilpah (Servant of Leah) (Gen. 29:24)
Gad (Gen. 30:11)
Tribe of Gad
Page 9
Asher (Gen. 30:13)
Tribe of Asher
Page 9
Jacob (Gen. 25:26) Israel (Gen. 32:28)
& Rachel (Gen 29:16)
Joseph (Gen. 30:24)
& Asenath (Gen. 41:45)
Tribes of Joseph
Page 13
Benjamin (Ben-Oni) (Gen. 35:18)
Tribe of Benjamin
Page 15
Rachel died giving birth to Benjamin. Genesis 35:16
Rachel is buried on the way to Ephrath (that is Bethlehem). Gen. 35:19 or in Ephron's field Gen. 49:39
Jacob lived 147 years and died while in Egypt, his bones were carried to the land of Canaan and buried in the cave in Ephron's field. Genesis 49:29,50:1-14
Gray Shadow
Denotes one of the
12 Tribes of Israel (Jacob)
Dinah (Gen. 30:21)
She was violated by Shechem, for which crime, Levi and Simeon destroyed the city. (Gen 34)
Jacob (Gen. 25:26) Israel (Gen. 32:28)
& Leah (Gen 29:16)
Reuben (Gen. 29:32)
Tribe of Reuben
Page 22
Issachar (Gen. 30:18)
Tribe of Issachar
Page 23
Zebulun (Gen. 30:20)
Tribe of Zebulun
Page 22
Simeon (Gen. 29:32)
Tribe of Simeon
Page 25
Levi (Gen 29:34)
Tribe of Levi
Page 27
Judah (Gen. 29:35)
& Bathshua (Gen. 38:2)
Tribe of Judah
Page 35
Judah (Gen. 29:35)
& Tamar (Gen. 38:6)
As the priestly Tribe, LEVI was given no land. Instead of land, God gave Levi the tithes of the people of Israel. JOSEPH had two sons MANASSEH and EPHRAIM. By Jacob's command, Joseph's sons, MANASSEH and EPHRAIM, were regarded as de facto "Tribes" of Israel. Thus, land allocations of Joseph and Levi were given to Ephraim and Manasseh, preserving "twelve"as the number of tribes. (Josh 14:3-4)

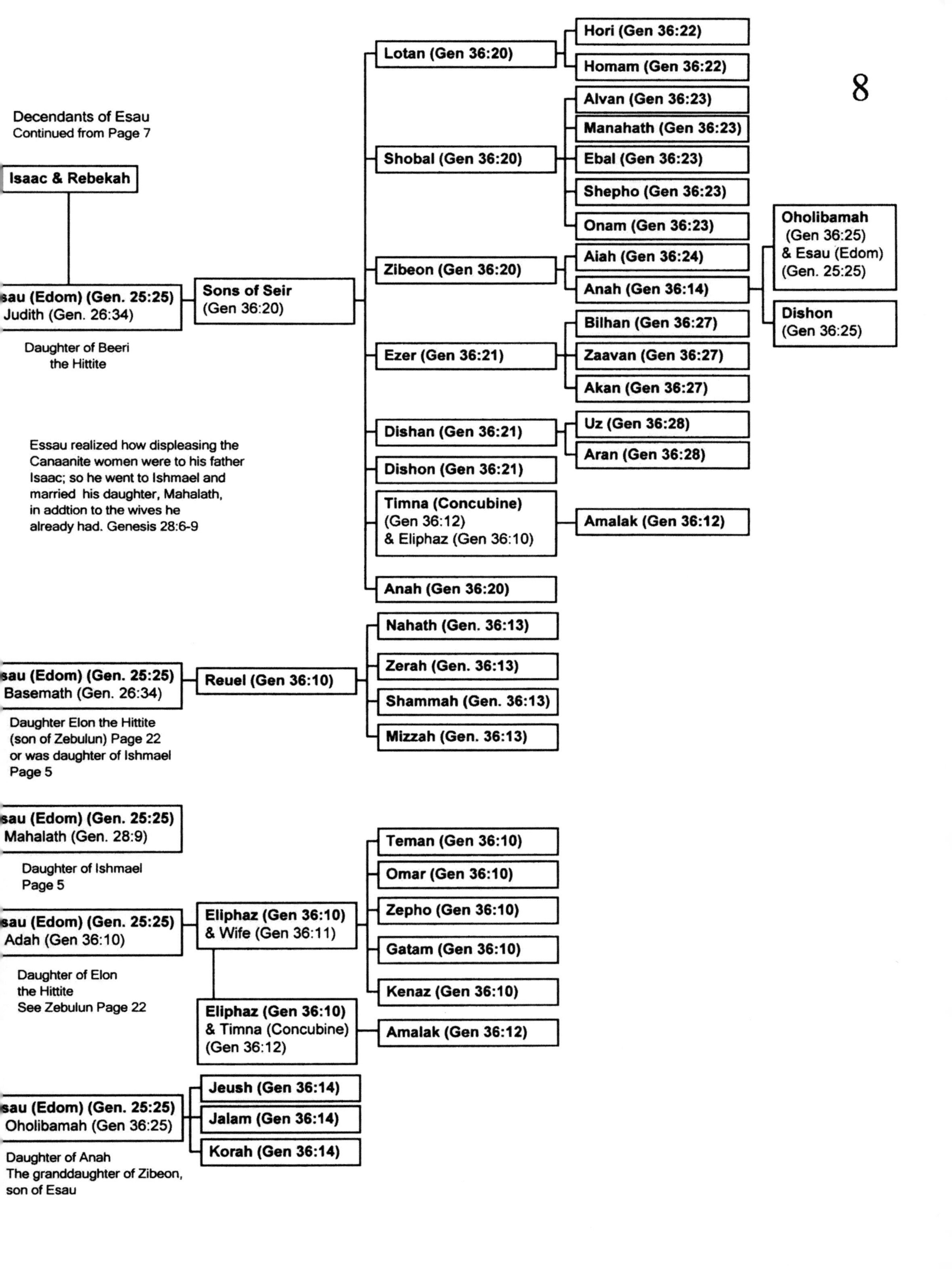
Decendants of Esau
Continued from Page 7
Isaac & Rebekah
sau (Edom) (Gen. 25:25)
Judith (Gen. 26:34)
Daughter of Beeri
the Hittite
Sons of Seir
(Gen 36:20)
Lotan (Gen 36:20)
Hori (Gen 36:22)
Homam (Gen 36:22)
Shobal (Gen 36:20)
Alvan (Gen 36:23)
Manahath (Gen 36:23)
Ebal (Gen 36:23)
Shepho (Gen 36:23)
Onam (Gen 36:23)
Zibeon (Gen 36:20)
Aiah (Gen 36:24)
Anah (Gen 36:14)
Oholibamah
(Gen 36:25)
& Esau (Edom)
(Gen. 25:25)
Dishon
(Gen 36:25)
Ezer (Gen 36:21)
Bilhan (Gen 36:27)
Zaavan (Gen 36:27)
Akan (Gen 36:27)
Dishan (Gen 36:21)
Uz (Gen 36:28)
Aran (Gen 36:28)
Dishon (Gen 36:21)
Timna (Concubine)
(Gen 36:12)
& Eliphaz (Gen 36:10)
Amalak (Gen 36:12)
Anah (Gen 36:20)
Essau realized how displeasing the
Canaanite women were to his father
Isaac; so he went to Ishmael and
married his daughter, Mahalath,
in addtion to the wives he
already had. Genesis 28:6-9
sau (Edom) (Gen. 25:25)
Basemath (Gen. 26:34)
Reuel (Gen 36:10)
Nahath (Gen. 36:13)
Zerah (Gen. 36:13)
Shammah (Gen. 36:13)
Mizzah (Gen. 36:13)
Daughter Elon the Hittite
(son of Zebulun) Page 22
or was daughter of Ishmael
Page 5
sau (Edom) (Gen. 25:25)
Mahalath (Gen. 28:9)
Daughter of Ishmael
Page 5
sau (Edom) (Gen. 25:25)
Adah (Gen 36:10)
Eliphaz (Gen 36:10)
& Wife (Gen 36:11)
Teman (Gen 36:10)
Omar (Gen 36:10)
Zepho (Gen 36:10)
Gatam (Gen 36:10)
Kenaz (Gen 36:10)
Daughter of Elon
the Hittite
See Zebulun Page 22
Eliphaz (Gen 36:10)
& Timna (Concubine)
(Gen 36:12)
Amalak (Gen 36:12)
sau (Edom) (Gen. 25:25)
Oholibamah (Gen 36:25)
Jeush (Gen 36:14)
Jalam (Gen 36:14)
Korah (Gen 36:14)
Daughter of Anah
The granddaughter of Zibeon,
son of Esau

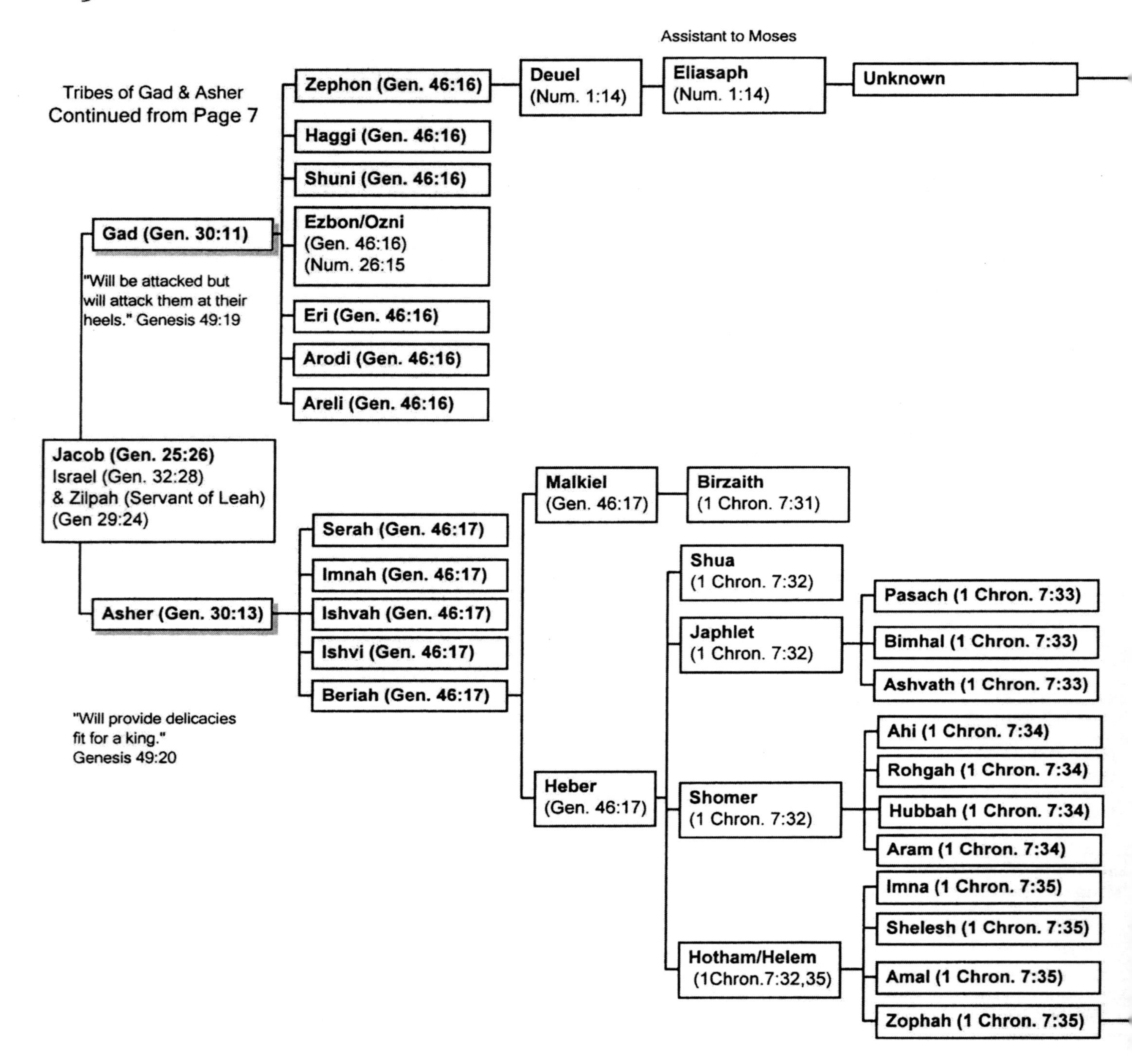
Tribes of Gad & Asher
Continued from Page 7
Assistant to Moses
Zephon (Gen. 46:16)
Deuel (Num. 1:14)
Eliasaph (Num. 1:14)
Unknown
Haggi (Gen. 46:16)
Shuni (Gen. 46:16)
Gad (Gen. 30:11)
Ezbon/Ozni (Gen. 46:16) (Num. 26:15
"Will be attacked but will attack them at their heels." Genesis 49:19
Eri (Gen. 46:16)
Arodi (Gen. 46:16)
Areli (Gen. 46:16)
Jacob (Gen. 25:26) Israel (Gen. 32:28) & Zilpah (Servant of Leah) (Gen 29:24)
Malkiel (Gen. 46:17)
Birzaith (1 Chron. 7:31)
Serah (Gen. 46:17)
Imnah (Gen. 46:17)
Asher (Gen. 30:13)
Ishvah (Gen. 46:17)
Ishvi (Gen. 46:17)
Beriah (Gen. 46:17)
Shua (1 Chron. 7:32)
Japhlet (1 Chron. 7:32)
Pasach (1 Chron. 7:33)
Bimhal (1 Chron. 7:33)
Ashvath (1 Chron. 7:33)
"Will provide delicacies fit for a king." Genesis 49:20
Heber (Gen. 46:17)
Shomer (1 Chron. 7:32)
Ahi (1 Chron. 7:34)
Rohgah (1 Chron. 7:34)
Hubbah (1 Chron. 7:34)
Aram (1 Chron. 7:34)
Hotham/Helem (1Chron.7:32,35)
Imna (1 Chron. 7:35)
Shelesh (1 Chron. 7:35)
Amal (1 Chron. 7:35)
Zophah (1 Chron. 7:35)

Buz (1 Chron. 5:14) — Jahdo (1 Chron. 5:14) — Jeshishai (1 Chron. 5:14)

Continued Page 11

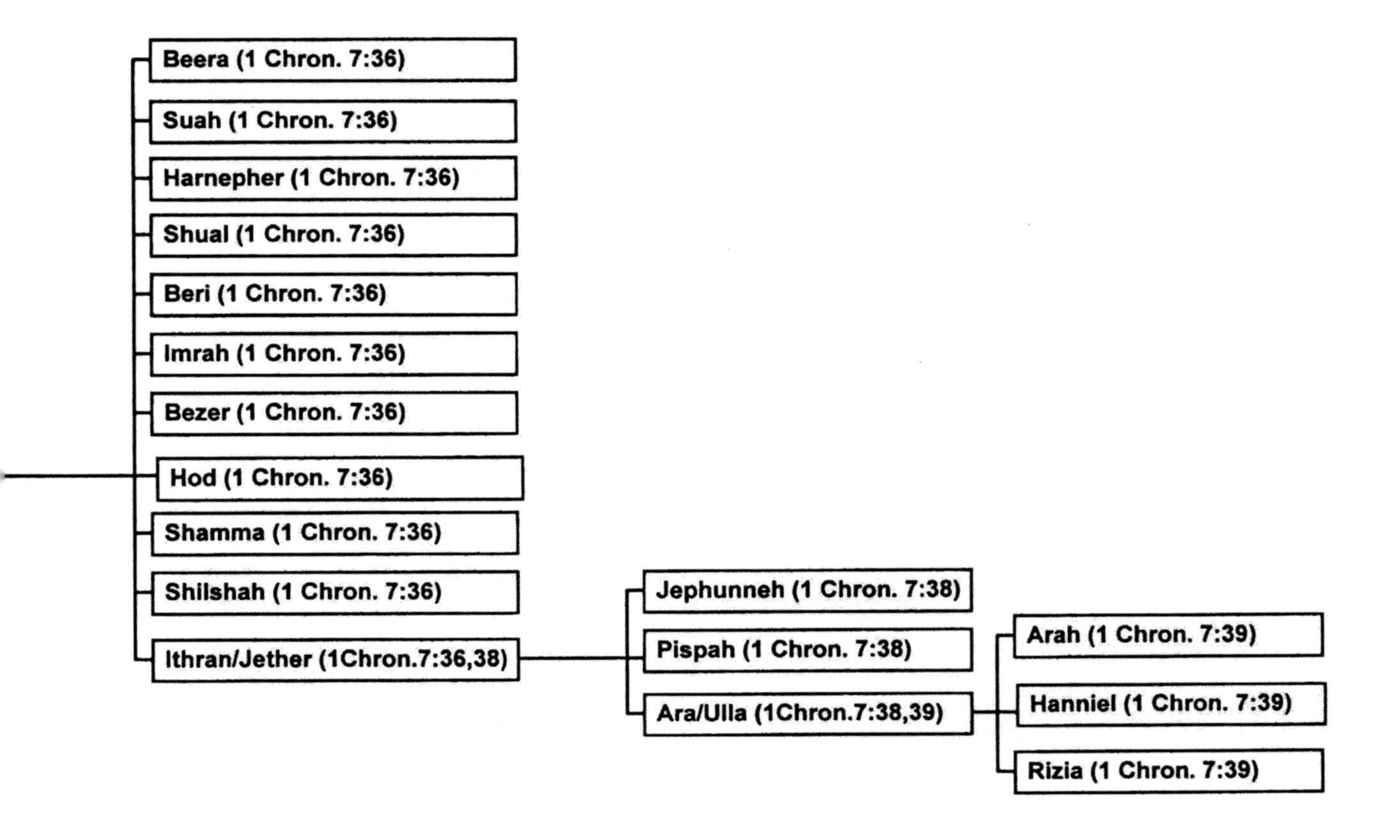
Beera (1 Chron. 7:36)
Suah (1 Chron. 7:36)
Harnepher (1 Chron. 7:36)
Shual (1 Chron. 7:36)
Beri (1 Chron. 7:36)
Imrah (1 Chron. 7:36)
Bezer (1 Chron. 7:36)
Hod (1 Chron. 7:36)
Shamma (1 Chron. 7:36)
Shilshah (1 Chron. 7:36)
Ithran/Jether (1Chron.7:36,38)
Jephunneh (1 Chron. 7:38)
Pispah (1 Chron. 7:38)
Ara/Ulla (1Chron.7:38,39)
Arah (1 Chron. 7:39)
Hanniel (1 Chron. 7:39)
Rizia (1 Chron. 7:39)

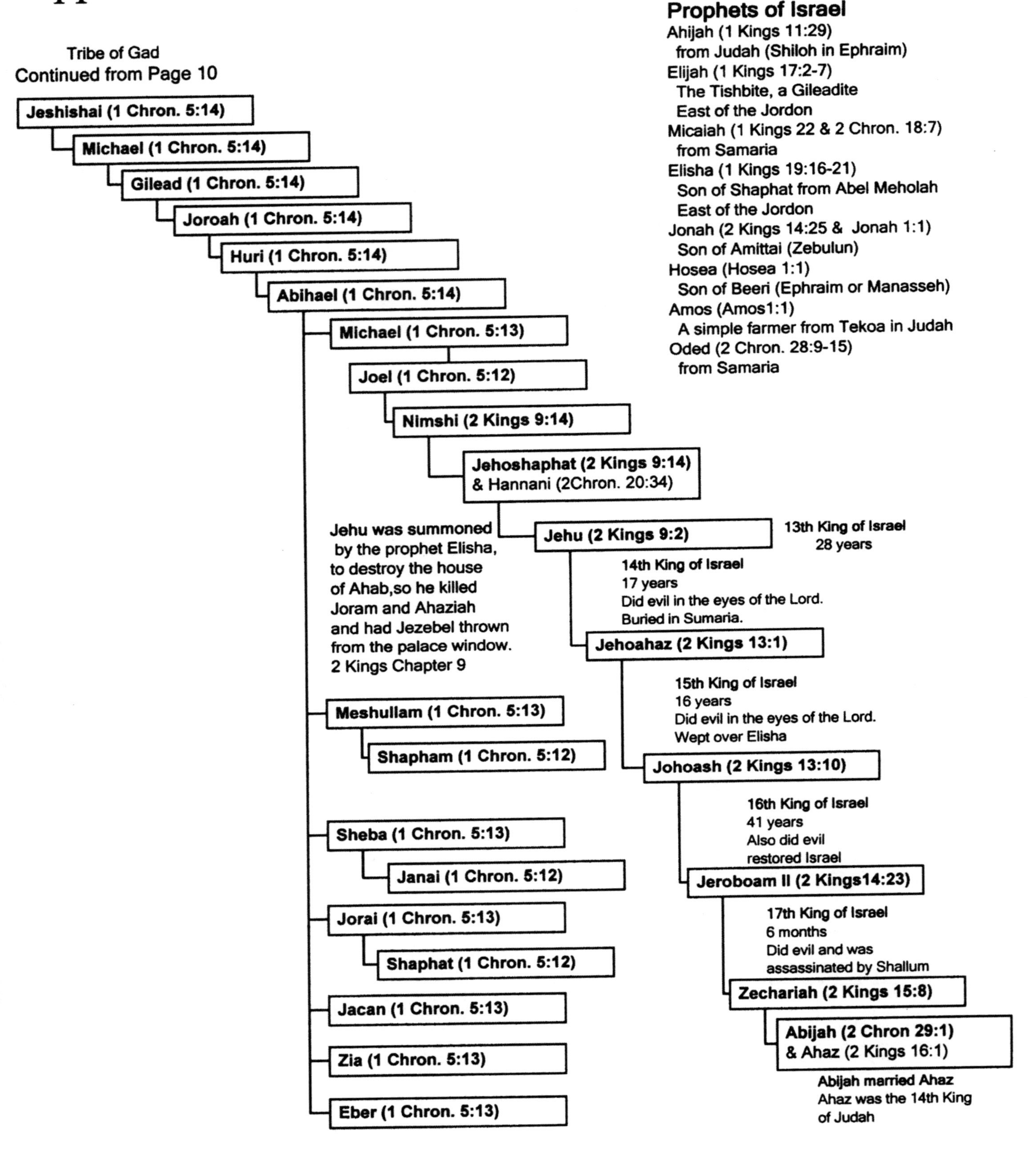
Tribe of Gad
Continued from Page 10
Jeshishai (1 Chron. 5:14)
Michael (1 Chron. 5:14)
Gilead (1 Chron. 5:14)
Joroah (1 Chron. 5:14)
Huri (1 Chron. 5:14)
Abihael (1 Chron. 5:14)
Michael (1 Chron. 5:13)
Joel (1 Chron. 5:12)
Nimshi (2 Kings 9:14)
Jehoshaphat (2 Kings 9:14) & Hannani (2Chron. 20:34)
Jehu was summoned by the prophet Elisha, to destroy the house of Ahab,so he killed Joram and Ahaziah and had Jezebel thrown from the palace window. 2 Kings Chapter 9
Jehu (2 Kings 9:2)
13th King of Israel 28 years
14th King of Israel
17 years
Did evil in the eyes of the Lord.
Buried in Sumaria.
Jehoahaz (2 Kings 13:1)
15th King of Israel
16 years
Did evil in the eyes of the Lord.
Wept over Elisha
Johoash (2 Kings 13:10)
16th King of Israel
41 years
Also did evil
restored Israel
Jeroboam II (2 Kings14:23)
17th King of Israel
6 months
Did evil and was
assassinated by Shallum
Zechariah (2 Kings 15:8)
Abijah (2 Chron 29:1) & Ahaz (2 Kings 16:1)
Abijah married Ahaz
Ahaz was the 14th King of Judah
Meshullam (1 Chron. 5:13)
Shapham (1 Chron. 5:12)
Sheba (1 Chron. 5:13)
Janai (1 Chron. 5:12)
Jorai (1 Chron. 5:13)
Shaphat (1 Chron. 5:12)
Jacan (1 Chron. 5:13)
Zia (1 Chron. 5:13)
Eber (1 Chron. 5:13)

Prophets of Israel

Ahijah (1 Kings 11:29)
from Judah (Shiloh in Ephraim)
Elijah (1 Kings 17:2-7)
The Tishbite, a Gileadite
East of the Jordon
Micaiah (1 Kings 22 & 2 Chron. 18:7)
from Samaria
Elisha (1 Kings 19:16-21)
Son of Shaphat from Abel Meholah
East of the Jordon
Jonah (2 Kings 14:25 & Jonah 1:1)
Son of Amittai (Zebulun)
Hosea (Hosea 1:1)
Son of Beeri (Ephraim or Manasseh)
Amos (Amos1:1)
A simple farmer from Tekoa in Judah
Oded (2 Chron. 28:9-15)
from Samaria

Tribes of Dan and Naphtali
Continued from Page 7

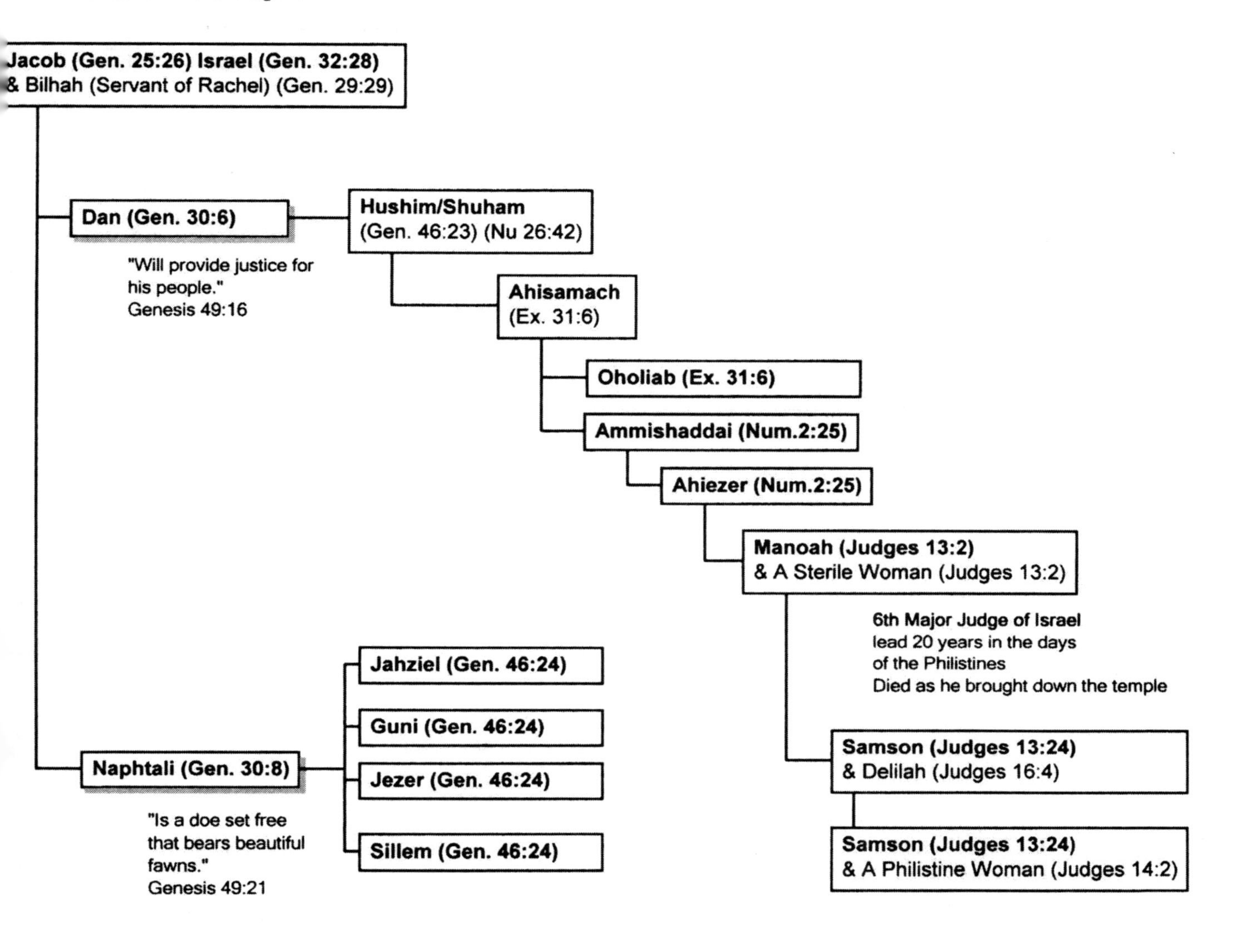

Jacob (Gen. 25:26) Israel (Gen. 32:28)
& Bilhah (Servant of Rachel) (Gen. 29:29)
Dan (Gen. 30:6)
"Will provide justice for his people." Genesis 49:16
Hushim/Shuham (Gen. 46:23) (Nu 26:42)
Ahisamach (Ex. 31:6)
Oholiab (Ex. 31:6)
Ammishaddai (Num.2:25)
Ahiezer (Num.2:25)
Manoah (Judges 13:2)
& A Sterile Woman (Judges 13:2)
6th Major Judge of Israel
lead 20 years in the days
of the Philistines
Died as he brought down the temple
Samson (Judges 13:24)
& Delilah (Judges 16:4)
Samson (Judges 13:24)
& A Philistine Woman (Judges 14:2)
Jahziel (Gen. 46:24)
Guni (Gen. 46:24)
Naphtali (Gen. 30:8)
Jezer (Gen. 46:24)
Sillem (Gen. 46:24)
"Is a doe set free that bears beautiful fawns." Genesis 49:21

Read about Samson
Judges Chapters 13-16

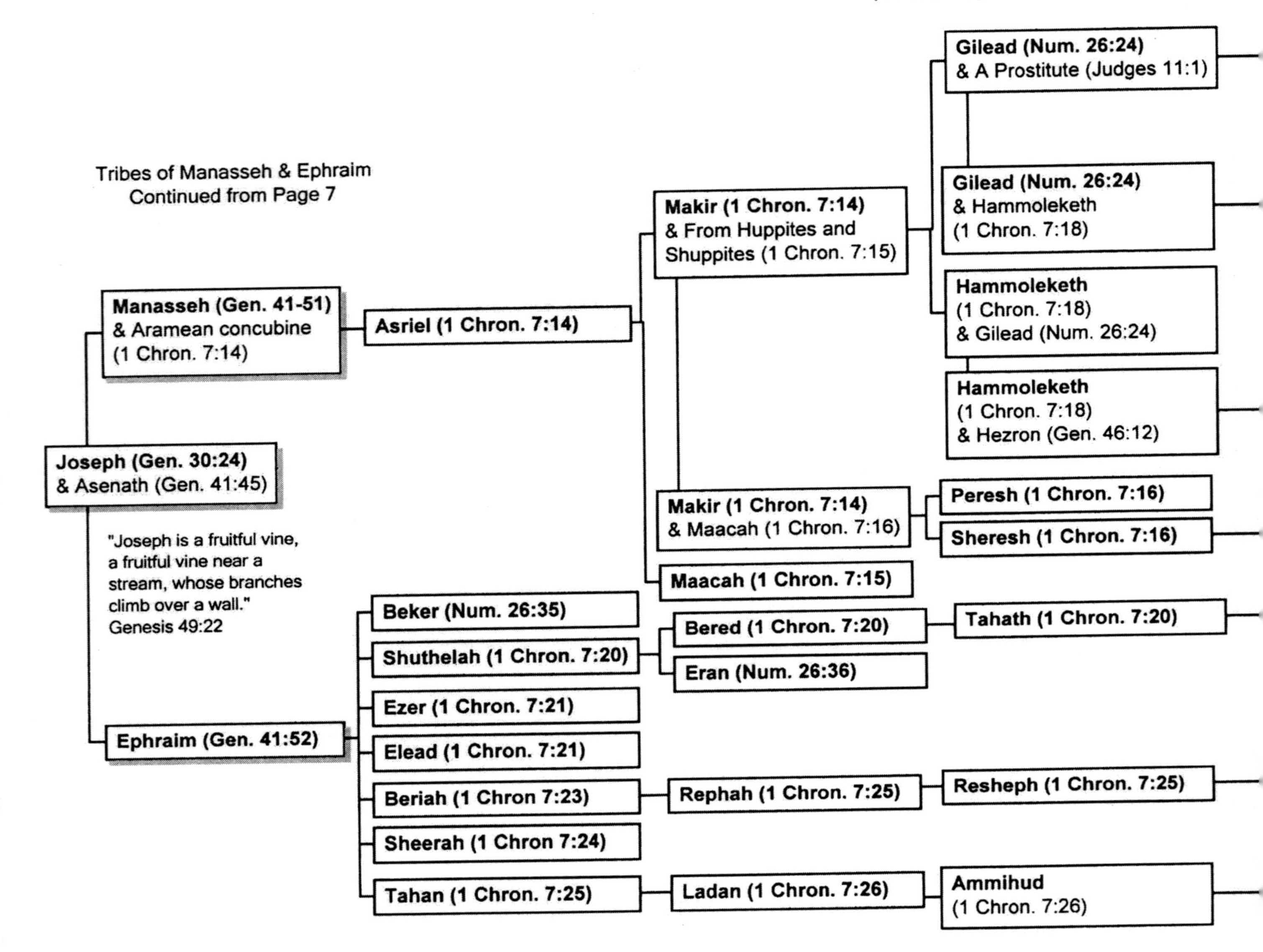
4th Major Judge of Israel, (Judges 4:5)
DEBORAH, Prophetess, wife of Lappidoth
Held court in the hill country of Ephraim
peace for 40 years.
Tribes of Manasseh & Ephraim
Continued from Page 7
Gilead (Num. 26:24)
& A Prostitute (Judges 11:1)
Gilead (Num. 26:24)
& Hammoleketh
(1 Chron. 7:18)
Makir (1 Chron. 7:14)
& From Huppites and
Shuppites (1 Chron. 7:15)
Hammoleketh
(1 Chron. 7:18)
& Gilead (Num. 26:24)
Manasseh (Gen. 41-51)
& Aramean concubine
(1 Chron. 7:14)
Asriel (1 Chron. 7:14)
Hammoleketh
(1 Chron. 7:18)
& Hezron (Gen. 46:12)
Joseph (Gen. 30:24)
& Asenath (Gen. 41:45)
Makir (1 Chron. 7:14)
& Maacah (1 Chron. 7:16)
Peresh (1 Chron. 7:16)
Sheresh (1 Chron. 7:16)
"Joseph is a fruitful vine,
a fruitful vine near a
stream, whose branches
climb over a wall."
Genesis 49:22
Maacah (1 Chron. 7:15)
Beker (Num. 26:35)
Bered (1 Chron. 7:20)
Tahath (1 Chron. 7:20)
Shuthelah (1 Chron. 7:20)
Eran (Num. 26:36)
Ezer (1 Chron. 7:21)
Ephraim (Gen. 41:52)
Elead (1 Chron. 7:21)
Beriah (1 Chron 7:23)
Rephah (1 Chron. 7:25)
Resheph (1 Chron. 7:25)
Sheerah (1 Chron 7:24)
Tahan (1 Chron. 7:25)
Ladan (1 Chron. 7:26)
Ammihud
(1 Chron. 7:26)

In later Years....
the last 5 kings of Israel
were possibly from the
Tribe of Manasseh

18th King of Israel
Shallum (2 Kings 15:13)
2 months, killed by Menahem

19th King of Israel
Menahem (Son of Gadi)
10 years, killed by Shallum
(2 Kings 15:17)

20th King of Israel
Pekahiah, Son of Manahem
2 years, killed by chief officer Pekah
(2 Kings 15:23)

21st King of Israel
Pekah (2 Kings 15:27)
20 years, killed by Hoshea

22nd King of Isreal
Hosea (2 Kings 17:1)
in 9th year, captured by Assyria

8th Major Judge
The son of a harlot, an outcast
He was a God fearing man.

Jephthah (Judges 11:1) — **Daughter (Judges 11:34)**

5th Major Judge
delivered Israel from the Midianites
with 300 men...Peace for 40 years.
Ended up worshipping Baal

Ishhod (1 Chron. 7:18)
Abiezer (1 Chron. 7:18) — **Joash (Judges 6:11)** — **Gideon (Jerub-Baal)** (Judges 6:11) & Many Wives (Judges 8:30) — **Jether (Judges 8:20)**, **70 Sons (Judges 8:30)**, **Jotham (Judges 9:5)**
Mahlah (1 Chron. 7:18)

Gideon (Jerub-Baal) (Judges 6:11) & Concubine in Shechem (Judges 8:31) — **Abimelech (Judges 8:31)**

6th Major Judge, Abimelech
Anti-Judge

Attempted to make
himself king but failed

Minor Judge, Jair
before Jephthah

Segub (1 Chron. 2:21) — **Jair (Judges 10:3)** — **30 Sons (Judges 10:3)**

Ulam (1 Chron. 7:16) — **Bedan (1 Chron. 7:17)**
Rakem (1 Chron. 7:16)

3rd Minor Judge after Jephthah
ABDON (Judges 12:13)
Son of Hillel, from Pirathon in
Ephraim. Had 40 sons & 30 grandsons !!!
8 years

Eleadah (1 Chron. 7:20) — **Tahath (1 Chron. 7:20)** & Shimeath (2Chron. 24:20) — **Zabad (1 Chron. 7:21)** — **Shuthelah (1 Chron. 7:21)**

Telah (1 Chron. 7:25)

God and Moses made Joshua their uncontested choice
for a new leader for Israel. Of all people that left Egypt,
only he and Caleb were allowed to enter the promised land.
Israel served the Lord throughout the lifetime of Joshua.

Elishama (Num.2:18) — **Nun (1 Chron. 7:26)** — **Joshua (Hosea)** (Joshua 1:1)

Kingdom of Israel formed (1Kings 11:31)
Jeroboam rebelled against Solomon
The prophet Ahija told him that he
would take ten pieces of the kingdom.
Idolatry became a part of the national religion.
All the kings of Israel were depraved and the
nations copied the conduct of their kings.

4th King of Israel
22 years
when the nation split after
death of Solomon.

5th King of Israel
2 years
did evil in the eyes
of the Lord

No connection
An Ephraimite from Zereda
(1Kings 11:26)

Nebat (1 Kings 12:2 Zeruah (1 Kings 11:26) — **Jeroboam (1 Kings 12:2)** — **Nadab (1 Kings 15:25)**, **Abijah (1 Kings 14:2)**

Tribe of Benjamin
Continued from Page 7

- **Benjamin (Ben-Oni)** (Gen. 35:18)
  - **Bela (Gen. 46:21)**
    - **Ezbon (1 Chron. 7:7)**
    - **Uzzi (1 Chron. 7:7)**
    - **Uzziel (1 Chron. 7:7)**
    - **Jerimoth (1 Chron. 7:7)**
    - **Ahoah/Iri (1 Chron. 8:4)** (1 Chron. 7:7)
      - **Shuppites (1 Chron. 7:12)**
      - **Huppites (1 Chron. 7:12)**
  - **Ashbel/Jadiael** (Gen. 46:21) (1Chron. 7:6)
    - **Bilhan (Hushites)** (1 Chron. 7:10)
      - **Jeush (1 Chron. 7:10)**
      - **Benjamin (1 Chron. 7:10)**
      - **Ehud (1 Chron. 7:10)**
      - **Kenaanah (1 Chron. 7:10)**
      - **Zethan (1 Chron. 7:10)**
      - **Tarshish (1 Chron. 7:10)**
      - **Ahishahar (1 Chron. 7:10)**
  - **Beker/Aharah** (Gen. 46:21) (1 Chron. 8:1)
    - **Zemirah (1 Chron. 7:8)**
    - **Joash (1 Chron. 7:8)**
    - **Elezer (1 Chron. 7:8)**
    - **Elioenai (1 Chron. 7:8)**
    - **Omri (1 Chron. 7:8)**
    - **Jeremoth (1 Chron. 7:8)**
    - **Abijah (1 Chron. 7:8)**
    - **Anathoth (1 Chron. 7:8)**
    - **Alemeth (1 Chron. 7:8)**
  - **Nohah (1 Chron. 8:2)**
  - **Rapha (1 Chron. 8:2)**
    - **4 decendants battle Israel** (2 Sam 21:15-22)

"Benjamin is a ravenous wolf in the morning he devours the prey, in the evening he divides the plunder." Genesis 49:27

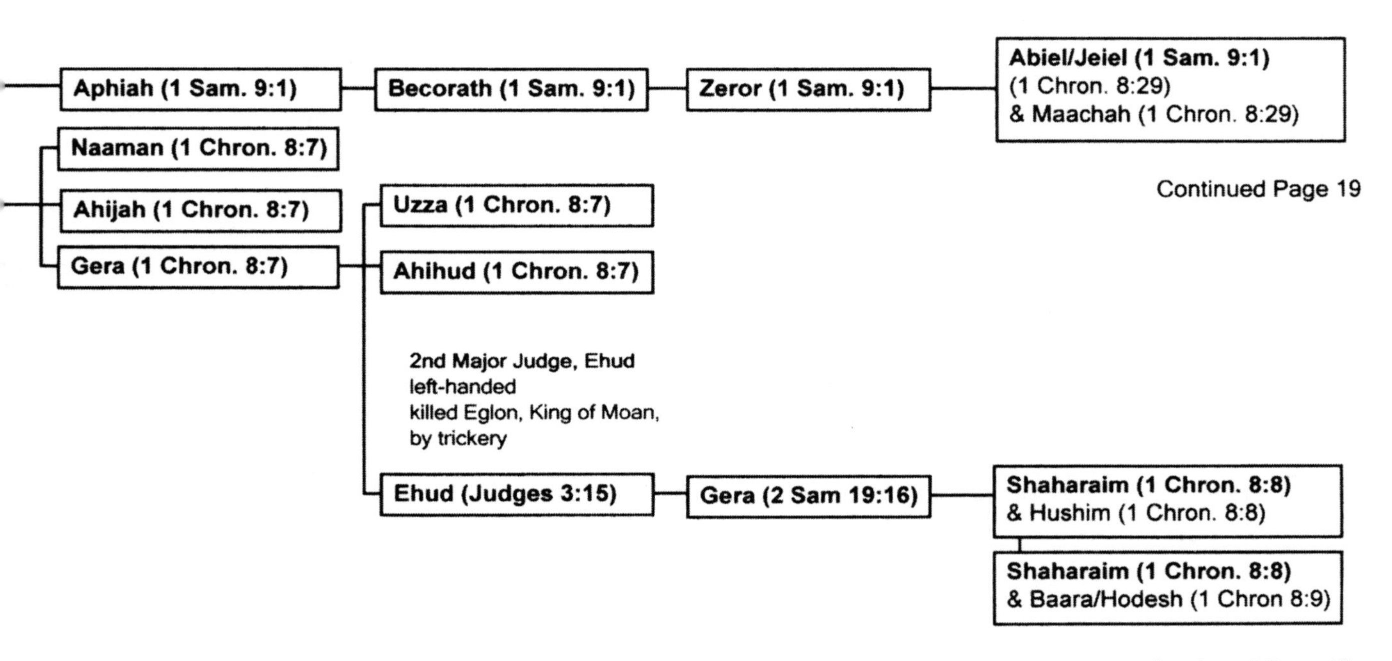

Aphiah (1 Sam. 9:1)
Becorath (1 Sam. 9:1)
Zeror (1 Sam. 9:1)
Abiel/Jeiel (1 Sam. 9:1)
(1 Chron. 8:29)
& Maachah (1 Chron. 8:29)
Naaman (1 Chron. 8:7)
Ahijah (1 Chron. 8:7)
Gera (1 Chron. 8:7)
Uzza (1 Chron. 8:7)
Ahihud (1 Chron. 8:7)
2nd Major Judge, Ehud
left-handed
killed Eglon, King of Moan,
by trickery
Ehud (Judges 3:15)
Gera (2 Sam 19:16)
Shaharaim (1 Chron. 8:8)
& Hushim (1 Chron. 8:8)
Shaharaim (1 Chron. 8:8)
& Baara/Hodesh (1 Chron 8:9)

Continued Page 19

Continued Page 17

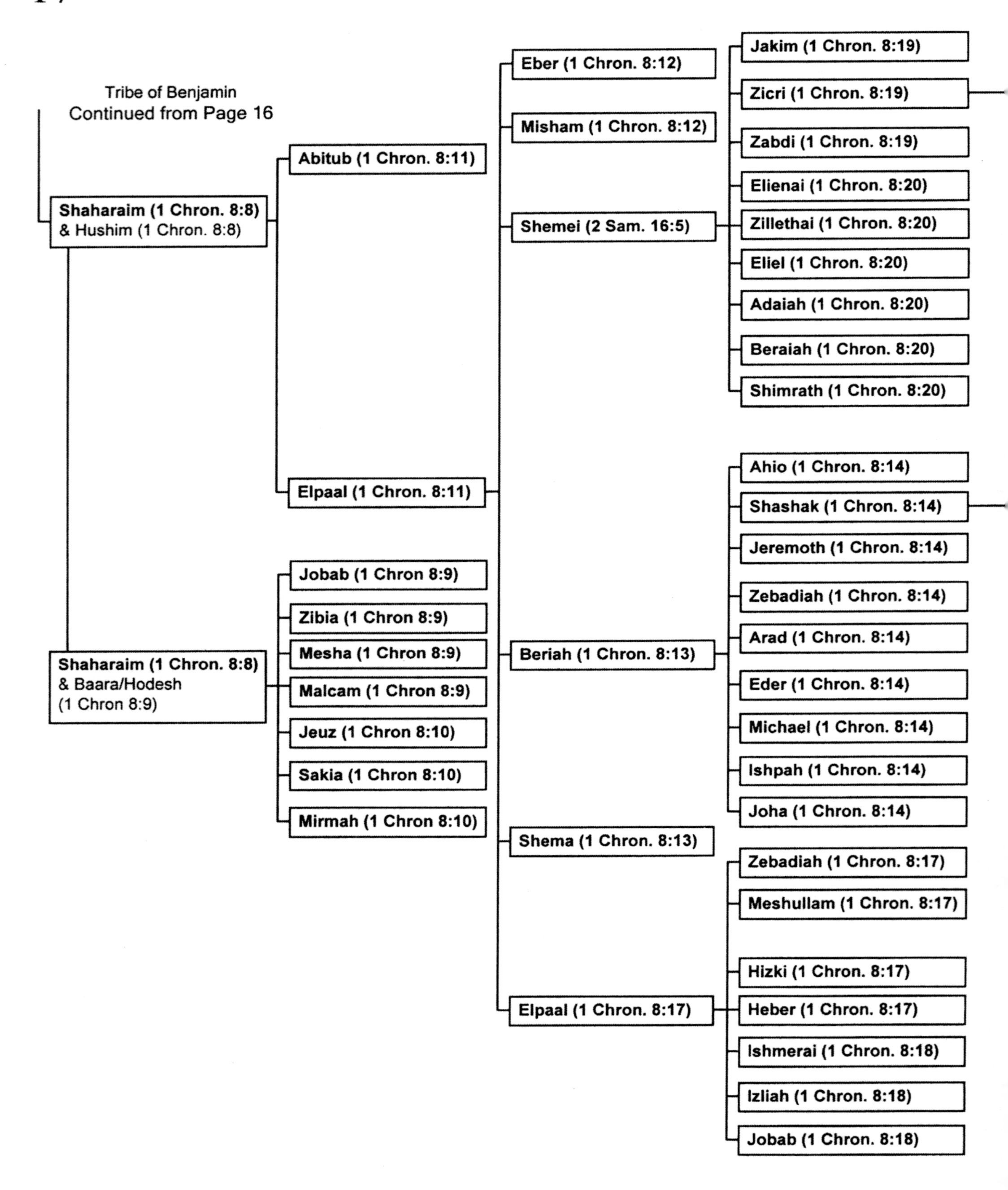
Tribe of Benjamin
Continued from Page 16
Shaharaim (1 Chron. 8:8) & Hushim (1 Chron. 8:8)
Abitub (1 Chron. 8:11)
Elpaal (1 Chron. 8:11)
Eber (1 Chron. 8:12)
Misham (1 Chron. 8:12)
Shemei (2 Sam. 16:5)
Jakim (1 Chron. 8:19)
Zicri (1 Chron. 8:19)
Zabdi (1 Chron. 8:19)
Elienai (1 Chron. 8:20)
Zillethai (1 Chron. 8:20)
Eliel (1 Chron. 8:20)
Adaiah (1 Chron. 8:20)
Beraiah (1 Chron. 8:20)
Shimrath (1 Chron. 8:20)
Beriah (1 Chron. 8:13)
Ahio (1 Chron. 8:14)
Shashak (1 Chron. 8:14)
Jeremoth (1 Chron. 8:14)
Zebadiah (1 Chron. 8:14)
Arad (1 Chron. 8:14)
Eder (1 Chron. 8:14)
Michael (1 Chron. 8:14)
Ishpah (1 Chron. 8:14)
Joha (1 Chron. 8:14)
Shema (1 Chron. 8:13)
Elpaal (1 Chron. 8:17)
Zebadiah (1 Chron. 8:17)
Meshullam (1 Chron. 8:17)
Hizki (1 Chron. 8:17)
Heber (1 Chron. 8:17)
Ishmerai (1 Chron. 8:18)
Izliah (1 Chron. 8:18)
Jobab (1 Chron. 8:18)
Shaharaim (1 Chron. 8:8) & Baara/Hodesh (1 Chron 8:9)
Jobab (1 Chron 8:9)
Zibia (1 Chron 8:9)
Mesha (1 Chron 8:9)
Malcam (1 Chron 8:9)
Jeuz (1 Chron 8:10)
Sakia (1 Chron 8:10)
Mirmah (1 Chron 8:10)

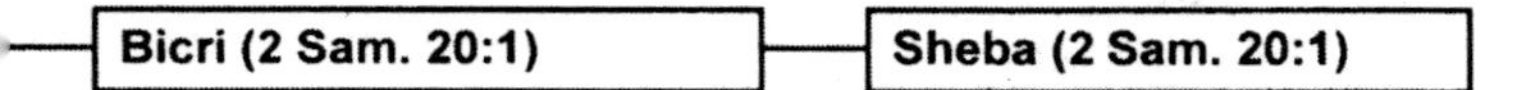
Bicri (2 Sam. 20:1)
Sheba (2 Sam. 20:1)

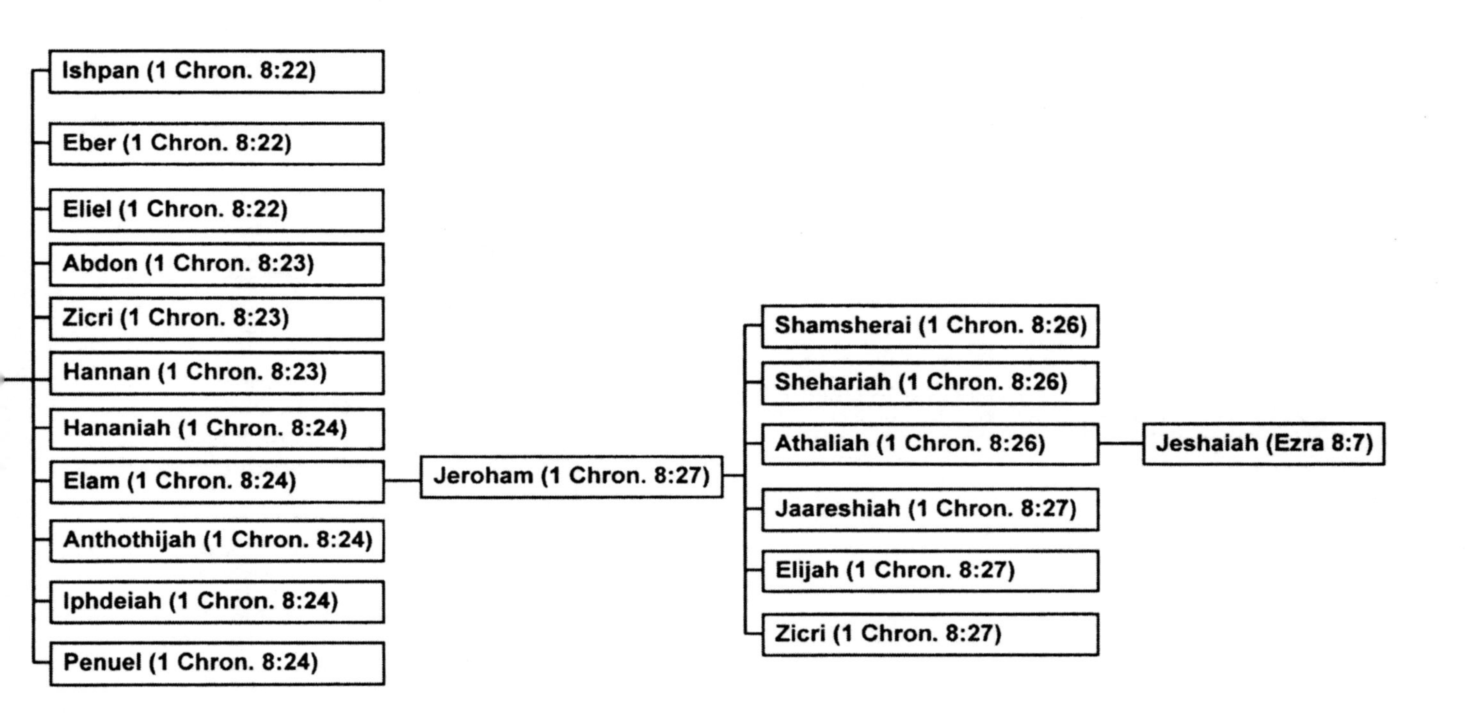
Ishpan (1 Chron. 8:22)
Eber (1 Chron. 8:22)
Eliel (1 Chron. 8:22)
Abdon (1 Chron. 8:23)
Zicri (1 Chron. 8:23)
Hannan (1 Chron. 8:23)
Hananiah (1 Chron. 8:24)
Elam (1 Chron. 8:24)
Anthothijah (1 Chron. 8:24)
Iphdeiah (1 Chron. 8:24)
Penuel (1 Chron. 8:24)
Jeroham (1 Chron. 8:27)
Shamsherai (1 Chron. 8:26)
Shehariah (1 Chron. 8:26)
Athaliah (1 Chron. 8:26)
Jaareshiah (1 Chron. 8:27)
Elijah (1 Chron. 8:27)
Zicri (1 Chron. 8:27)
Jeshaiah (Ezra 8:7)

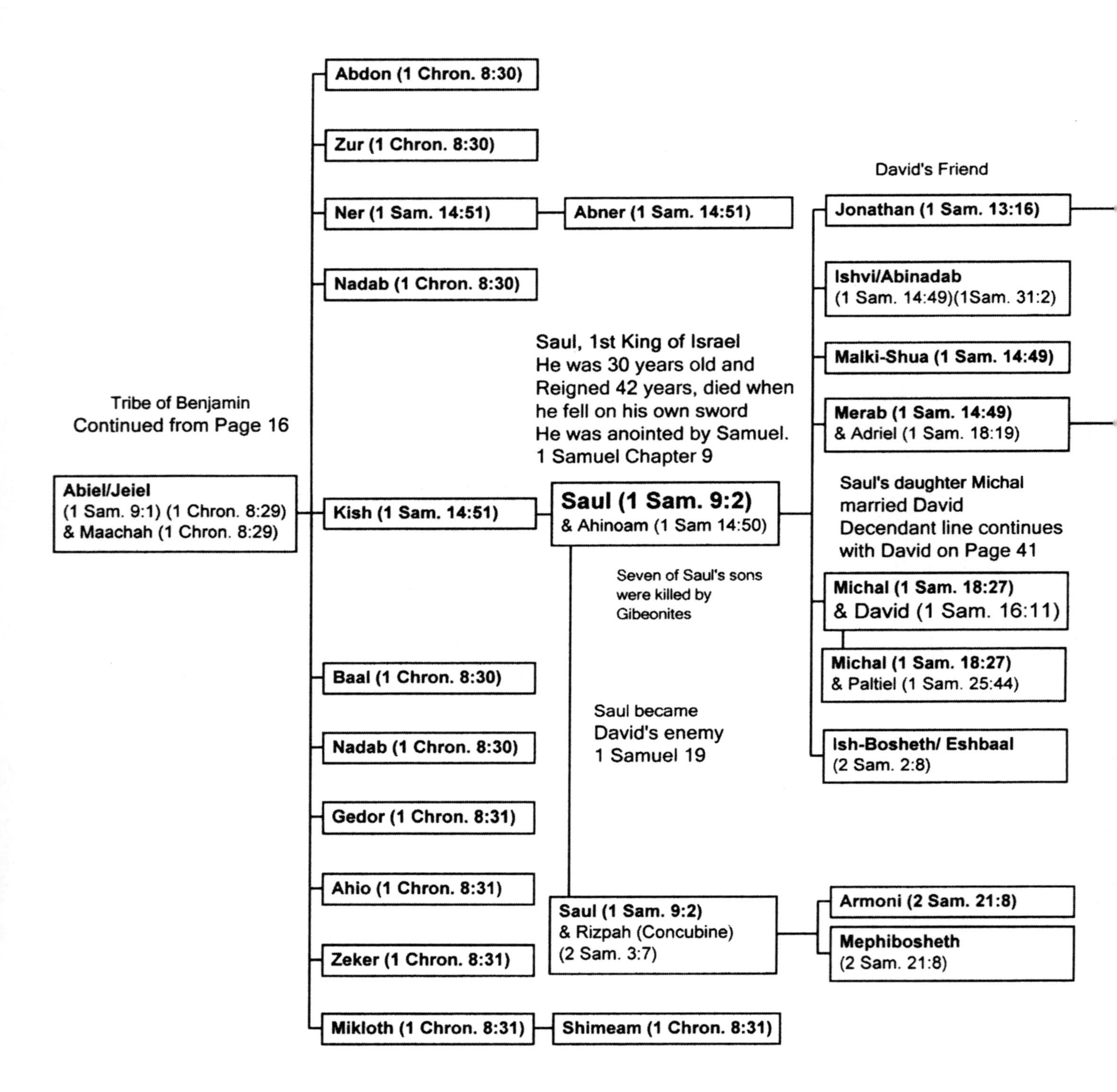
Abdon (1 Chron. 8:30)
Zur (1 Chron. 8:30)
David's Friend
Ner (1 Sam. 14:51)
Abner (1 Sam. 14:51)
Jonathan (1 Sam. 13:16)
Nadab (1 Chron. 8:30)
Ishvi/Abinadab (1 Sam. 14:49)(1Sam. 31:2)
Saul, 1st King of Israel
He was 30 years old and
Reigned 42 years, died when
he fell on his own sword
He was anointed by Samuel.
1 Samuel Chapter 9
Malki-Shua (1 Sam. 14:49)
Tribe of Benjamin
Continued from Page 16
Merab (1 Sam. 14:49)
& Adriel (1 Sam. 18:19)
Abiel/Jeiel
(1 Sam. 9:1) (1 Chron. 8:29)
& Maachah (1 Chron. 8:29)
Kish (1 Sam. 14:51)
Saul (1 Sam. 9:2)
& Ahinoam (1 Sam 14:50)
Saul's daughter Michal
married David
Decendant line continues
with David on Page 41
Seven of Saul's sons
were killed by
Gibeonites
Michal (1 Sam. 18:27)
& David (1 Sam. 16:11)
Michal (1 Sam. 18:27)
& Paltiel (1 Sam. 25:44)
Baal (1 Chron. 8:30)
Saul became
David's enemy
1 Samuel 19
Nadab (1 Chron. 8:30)
Ish-Bosheth/ Eshbaal
(2 Sam. 2:8)
Gedor (1 Chron. 8:31)
Ahio (1 Chron. 8:31)
Armoni (2 Sam. 21:8)
Saul (1 Sam. 9:2)
& Rizpah (Concubine)
(2 Sam. 3:7)
Mephibosheth
(2 Sam. 21:8)
Zeker (1 Chron. 8:31)
Mikloth (1 Chron. 8:31)
Shimeam (1 Chron. 8:31)

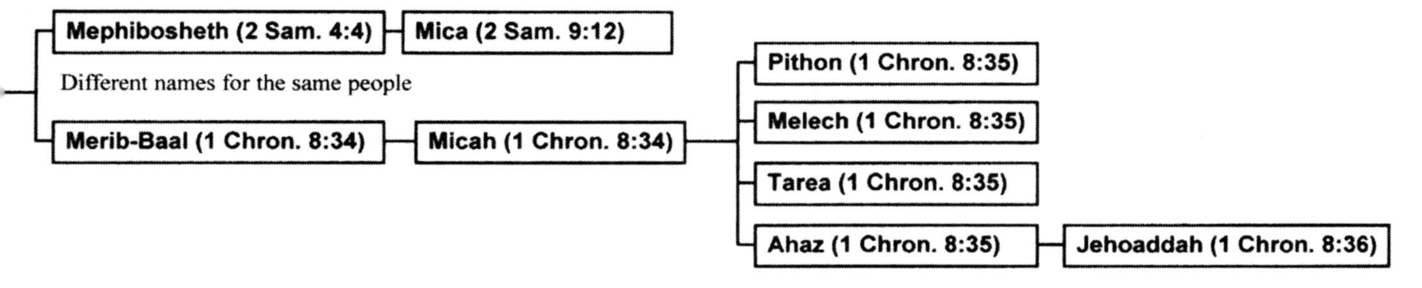
Went to live in the House of David, because when he was 5 years old his father was killed.
Mephibosheth (2 Sam. 4:4)
Mica (2 Sam. 9:12)
Different names for the same people
Merib-Baal (1 Chron. 8:34)
Micah (1 Chron. 8:34)
Pithon (1 Chron. 8:35)
Melech (1 Chron. 8:35)
Tarea (1 Chron. 8:35)
Ahaz (1 Chron. 8:35)
Jehoaddah (1 Chron. 8:36)

Continued Page 21

5 Sons (2 Sam. 21:8)

Tribe of Benjamin
Continued from Page 20

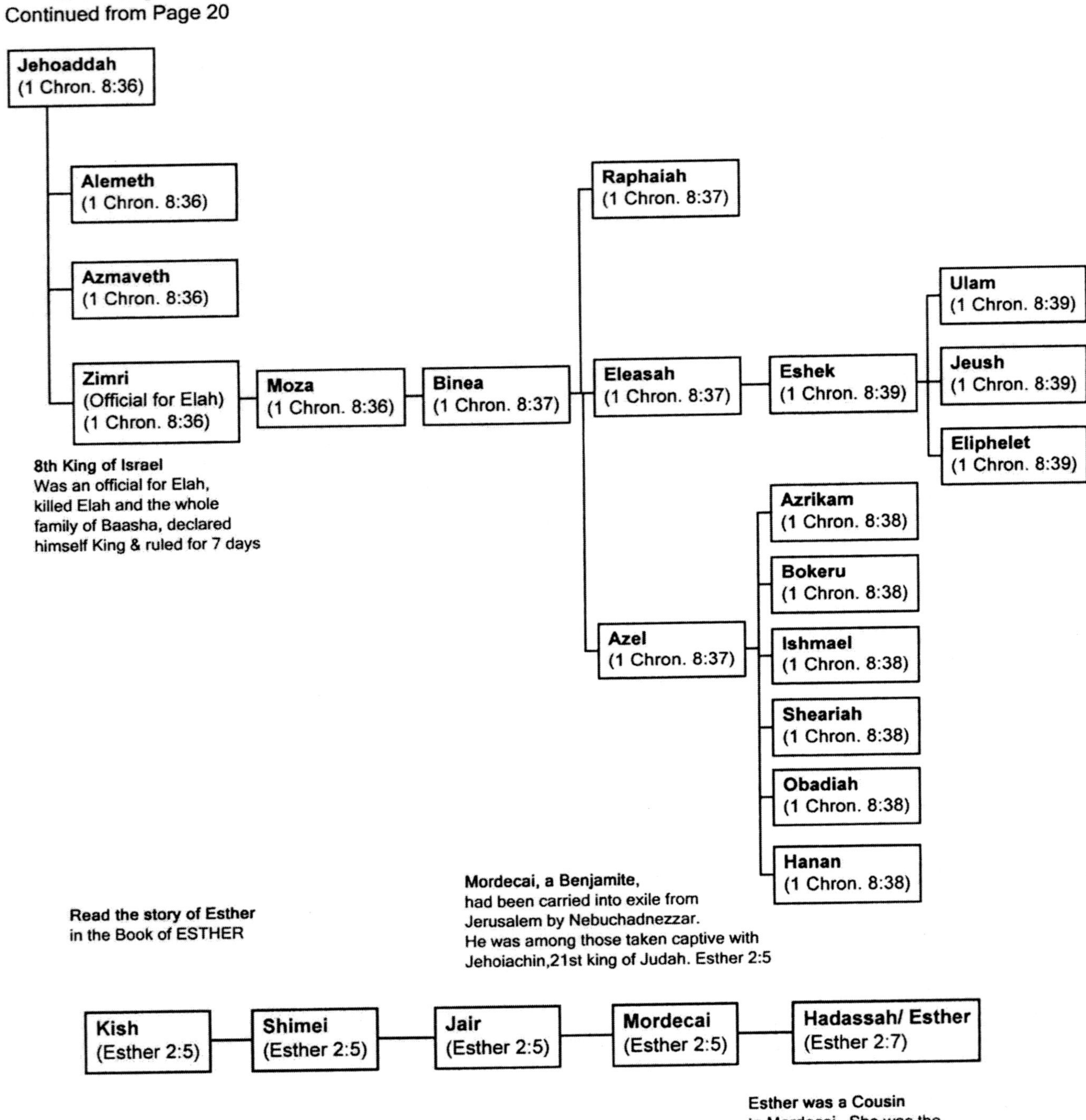
Jehoaddah (1 Chron. 8:36)
Alemeth (1 Chron. 8:36)
Azmaveth (1 Chron. 8:36)
Zimri (Official for Elah) (1 Chron. 8:36)
Moza (1 Chron. 8:36)
Binea (1 Chron. 8:37)
Raphaiah (1 Chron. 8:37)
Eleasah (1 Chron. 8:37)
Eshek (1 Chron. 8:39)
Ulam (1 Chron. 8:39)
Jeush (1 Chron. 8:39)
Eliphelet (1 Chron. 8:39)
Azel (1 Chron. 8:37)
Azrikam (1 Chron. 8:38)
Bokeru (1 Chron. 8:38)
Ishmael (1 Chron. 8:38)
Sheariah (1 Chron. 8:38)
Obadiah (1 Chron. 8:38)
Hanan (1 Chron. 8:38)
8th King of Israel
Was an official for Elah, killed Elah and the whole family of Baasha, declared himself King & ruled for 7 days
Read the story of Esther in the Book of ESTHER
Mordecai, a Benjamite, had been carried into exile from Jerusalem by Nebuchadnezzar. He was among those taken captive with Jehoiachin,21st king of Judah. Esther 2:5
Kish (Esther 2:5)
Shimei (Esther 2:5)
Jair (Esther 2:5)
Mordecai (Esther 2:5)
Hadassah/ Esther (Esther 2:7)
Esther was a Cousin to Mordecai. She was the daughter of his uncle Abihail. Mordecai took her for his own daughter. Esther 2:7,15

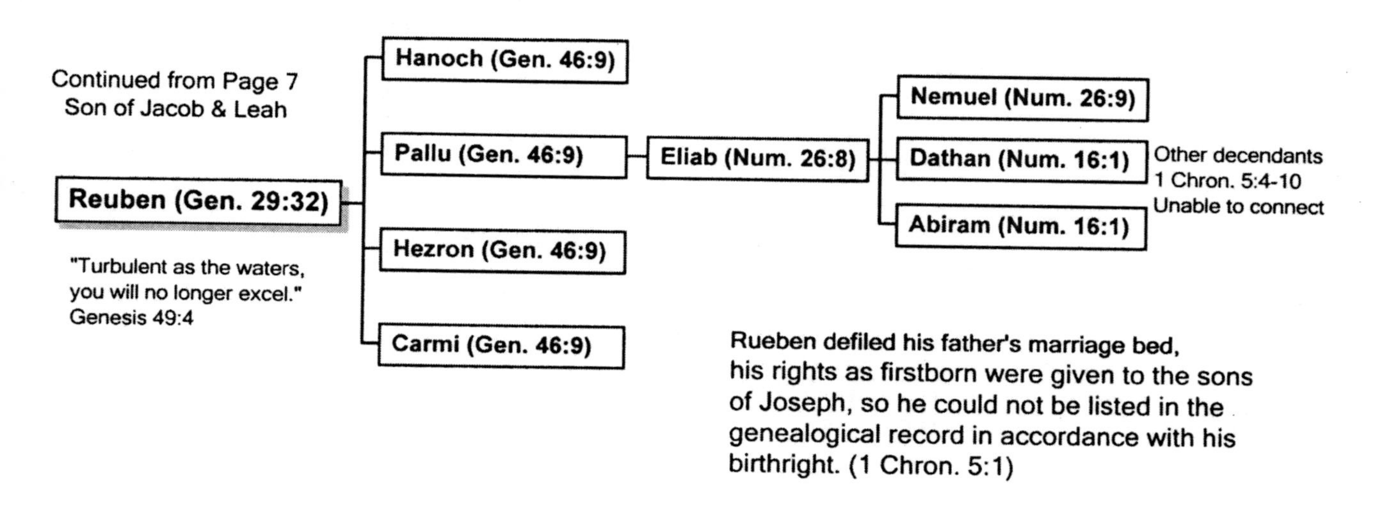
Continued from Page 7
Son of Jacob & Leah
Reuben (Gen. 29:32)
"Turbulent as the waters, you will no longer excel." Genesis 49:4
Hanoch (Gen. 46:9)
Pallu (Gen. 46:9)
Hezron (Gen. 46:9)
Carmi (Gen. 46:9)
Eliab (Num. 26:8)
Nemuel (Num. 26:9)
Dathan (Num. 16:1)
Abiram (Num. 16:1)
Other decendants
1 Chron. 5:4-10
Unable to connect

Rueben defiled his father's marriage bed, his rights as firstborn were given to the sons of Joseph, so he could not be listed in the genealogical record in accordance with his birthright. (1 Chron. 5:1)

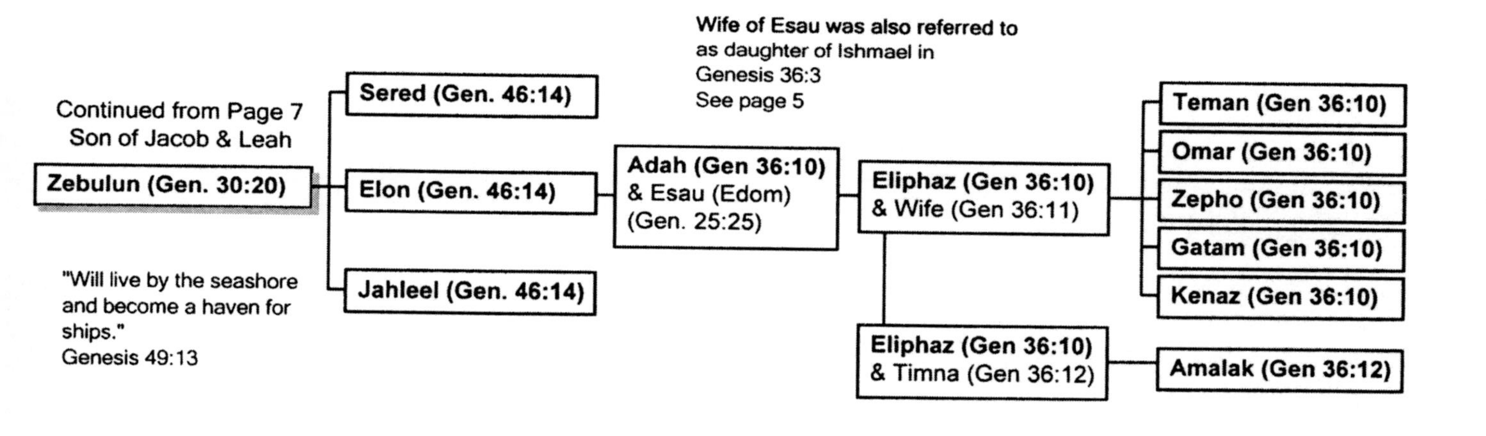
Wife of Esau was also referred to as daughter of Ishmael in Genesis 36:3
See page 5
Continued from Page 7
Son of Jacob & Leah
Zebulun (Gen. 30:20)
"Will live by the seashore and become a haven for ships." Genesis 49:13
Sered (Gen. 46:14)
Elon (Gen. 46:14)
Jahleel (Gen. 46:14)
Adah (Gen 36:10) & Esau (Edom) (Gen. 25:25)
Eliphaz (Gen 36:10) & Wife (Gen 36:11)
Eliphaz (Gen 36:10) & Timna (Gen 36:12)
Teman (Gen 36:10)
Omar (Gen 36:10)
Zepho (Gen 36:10)
Gatam (Gen 36:10)
Kenaz (Gen 36:10)
Amalak (Gen 36:12)

Ibzan (Judges 12:8-9
Minor Judge following Jephthah
30 sons and 30 daughters
Tribe of Zebulun

Elon (Judges 12:11-12
2nd Minor Judge following Jephthah
Ruled 10 years
Tribe of Zebulun

Tribe of Issachar
Continued from Page 7

Issachar (Gen. 30:18)

"Will submit to forced labor." Genesis 49:14

- **Tola (Gen. 46:13)**
  - **Uzzi** (1 Chron. 7:2)
    - **Izrahiah** (1 Chron. 7:3)
      - **Michael** (1 Chron. 7:3) — **Unknown** — **Unknown**
      - **Obadiah** (1 Chron. 7:3)
      - **Isshiah** (1 Chron. 7:3)
      - **Joel** (1 Chron. 7:3) — **Unknown** — **Unknown**
  - **Rephaiah** (1 Chron. 7:2)
  - **Jeriel** (1 Chron. 7:2)
  - **Jahmai** (1 Chron. 7:2)
  - **Ibsam** (1 Chron. 7:2)
  - **Samuel** (1 Chron. 7:2)
- **Puah (Gen. 46:13)** — **Unknown** — **Unknown** — **Unknown** — **Unknown** — **Unknown**
- **Jashub (Gen. 46:13)**
- **Shimron (Gen. 46:13)**

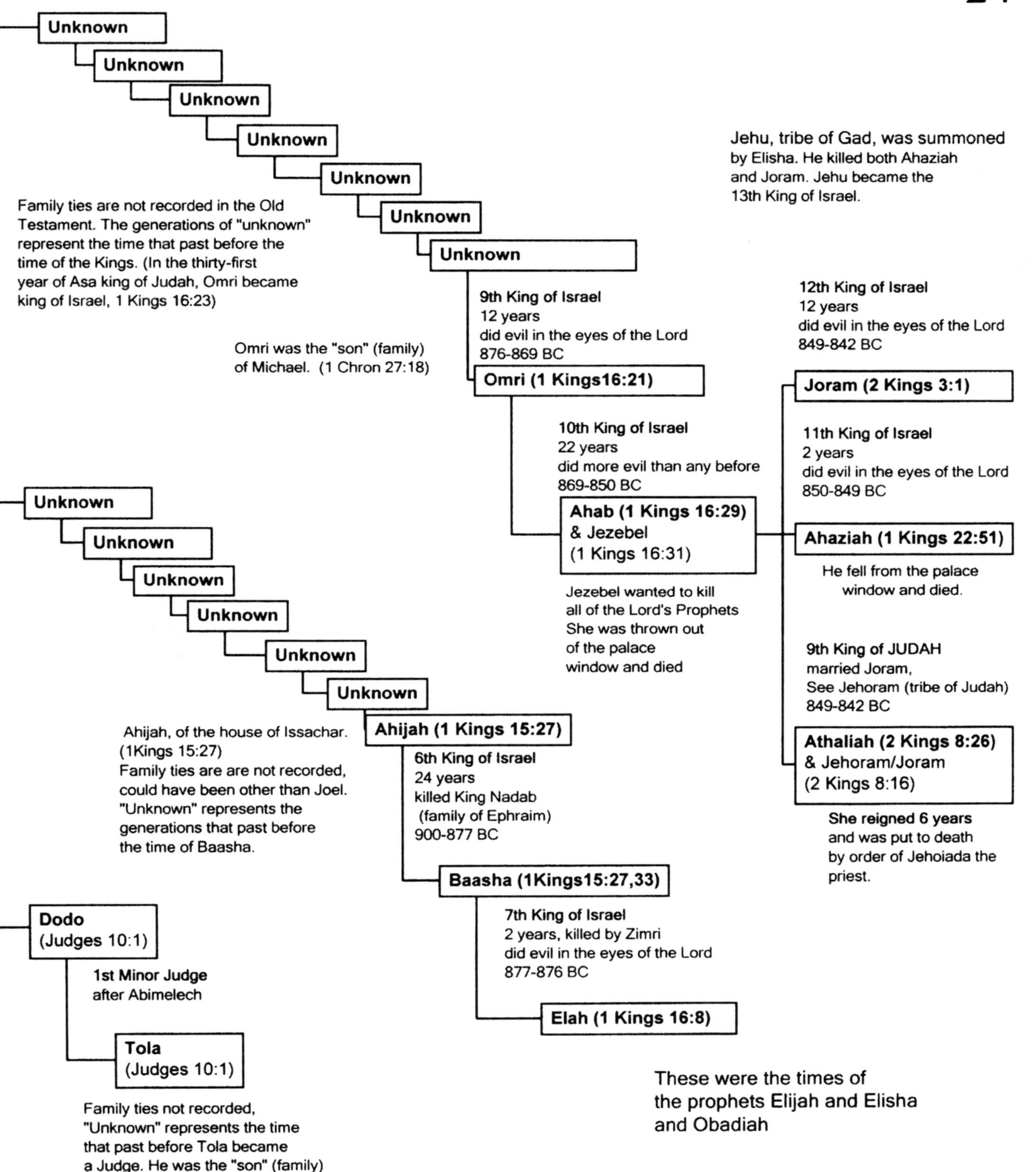
Unknown
Unknown
Unknown
Unknown
Unknown
Unknown
Unknown
Family ties are not recorded in the Old Testament. The generations of "unknown" represent the time that past before the time of the Kings. (In the thirty-first year of Asa king of Judah, Omri became king of Israel, 1 Kings 16:23)
Jehu, tribe of Gad, was summoned by Elisha. He killed both Ahaziah and Joram. Jehu became the 13th King of Israel.
9th King of Israel
12 years
did evil in the eyes of the Lord
876-869 BC
Omri was the "son" (family) of Michael. (1 Chron 27:18)
Omri (1 Kings16:21)
12th King of Israel
12 years
did evil in the eyes of the Lord
849-842 BC
Joram (2 Kings 3:1)
10th King of Israel
22 years
did more evil than any before
869-850 BC
11th King of Israel
2 years
did evil in the eyes of the Lord
850-849 BC
Ahab (1 Kings 16:29) & Jezebel (1 Kings 16:31)
Ahaziah (1 Kings 22:51)
He fell from the palace window and died.
Jezebel wanted to kill all of the Lord's Prophets She was thrown out of the palace window and died
Unknown
Unknown
Unknown
Unknown
Unknown
Unknown
9th King of JUDAH
married Joram,
See Jehoram (tribe of Judah)
849-842 BC
Ahijah (1 Kings 15:27)
Ahijah, of the house of Issachar. (1Kings 15:27)
Family ties are are not recorded, could have been other than Joel. "Unknown" represents the generations that past before the time of Baasha.
6th King of Israel
24 years
killed King Nadab
(family of Ephraim)
900-877 BC
Athaliah (2 Kings 8:26) & Jehoram/Joram (2 Kings 8:16)
She reigned 6 years and was put to death by order of Jehoiada the priest.
Baasha (1Kings15:27,33)
Dodo (Judges 10:1)
7th King of Israel
2 years, killed by Zimri
did evil in the eyes of the Lord
877-876 BC
1st Minor Judge
after Abimelech
Elah (1 Kings 16:8)
Tola (Judges 10:1)
These were the times of the prophets Elijah and Elisha and Obadiah
Family ties not recorded, "Unknown" represents the time that past before Tola became a Judge. He was the "son" (family) of Puah. (Judges 10:1)

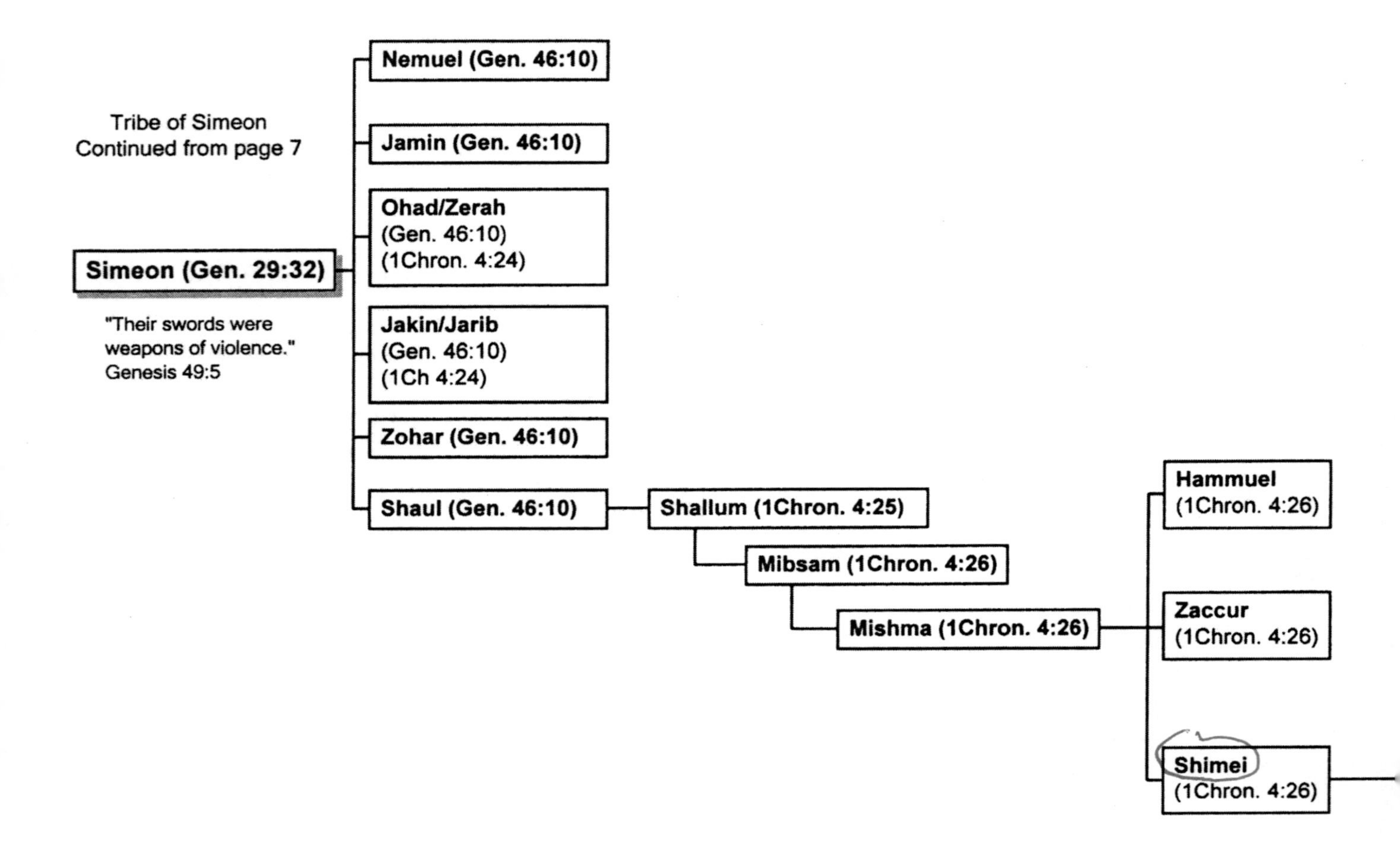
Tribe of Simeon
Continued from page 7
Simeon (Gen. 29:32)
"Their swords were weapons of violence." Genesis 49:5
Nemuel (Gen. 46:10)
Jamin (Gen. 46:10)
Ohad/Zerah (Gen. 46:10) (1Chron. 4:24)
Jakin/Jarib (Gen. 46:10) (1Ch 4:24)
Zohar (Gen. 46:10)
Shaul (Gen. 46:10)
Shallum (1Chron. 4:25)
Mibsam (1Chron. 4:26)
Mishma (1Chron. 4:26)
Hammuel (1Chron. 4:26)
Zaccur (1Chron. 4:26)
Shimei (1Chron. 4:26)

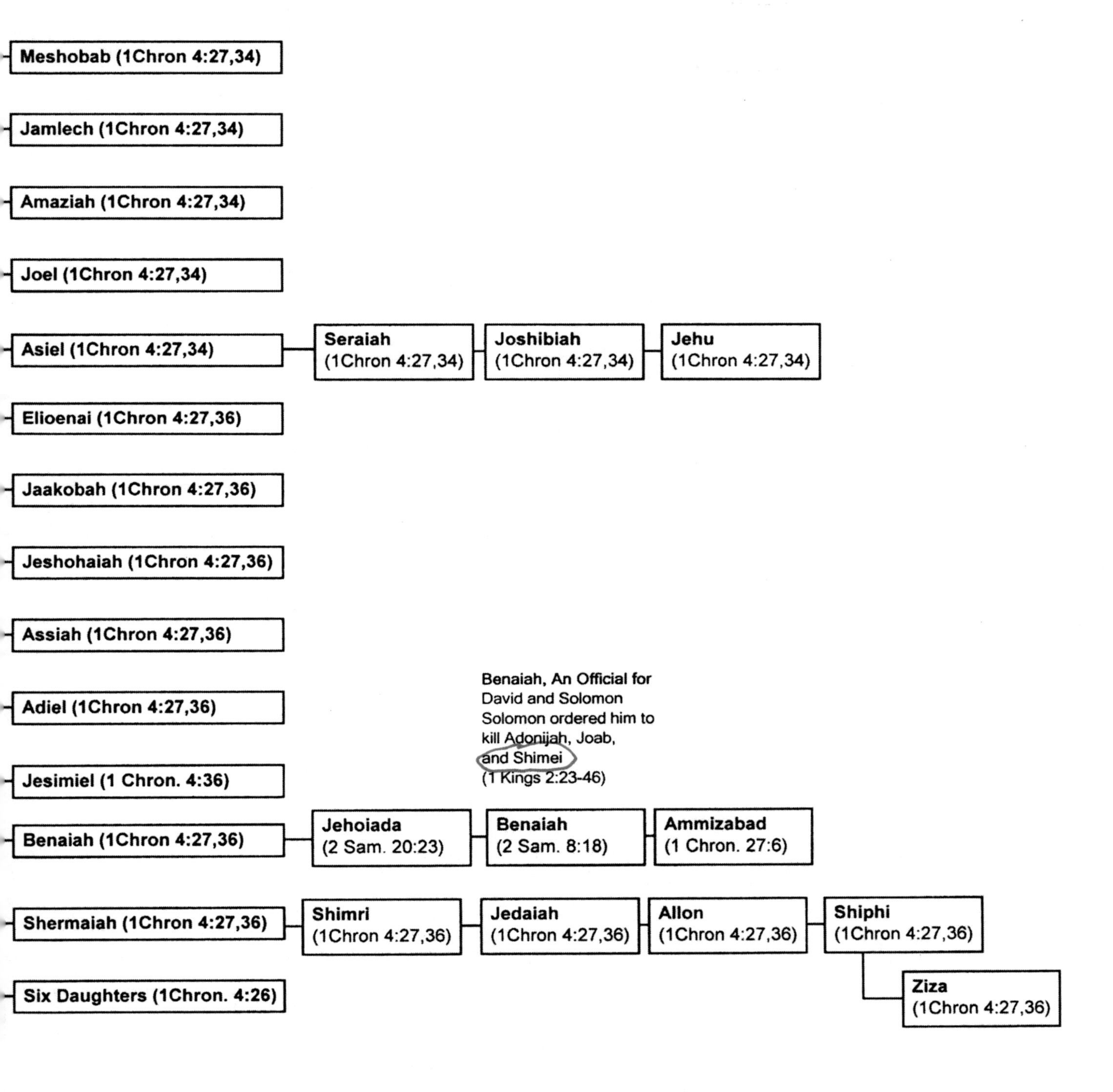

Meshobab (1Chron 4:27,34)
Jamlech (1Chron 4:27,34)
Amaziah (1Chron 4:27,34)
Joel (1Chron 4:27,34)
Asiel (1Chron 4:27,34)
Seraiah (1Chron 4:27,34)
Joshibiah (1Chron 4:27,34)
Jehu (1Chron 4:27,34)
Elioenai (1Chron 4:27,36)
Jaakobah (1Chron 4:27,36)
Jeshohaiah (1Chron 4:27,36)
Assiah (1Chron 4:27,36)
Adiel (1Chron 4:27,36)
Benaiah, An Official for David and Solomon Solomon ordered him to kill Adonijah, Joab, and Shimei (1 Kings 2:23-46)
Jesimiel (1 Chron. 4:36)
Benaiah (1Chron 4:27,36)
Jehoiada (2 Sam. 20:23)
Benaiah (2 Sam. 8:18)
Ammizabad (1 Chron. 27:6)
Shermaiah (1Chron 4:27,36)
Shimri (1Chron 4:27,36)
Jedaiah (1Chron 4:27,36)
Allon (1Chron 4:27,36)
Shiphi (1Chron 4:27,36)
Ziza (1Chron 4:27,36)
Six Daughters (1Chron. 4:26)

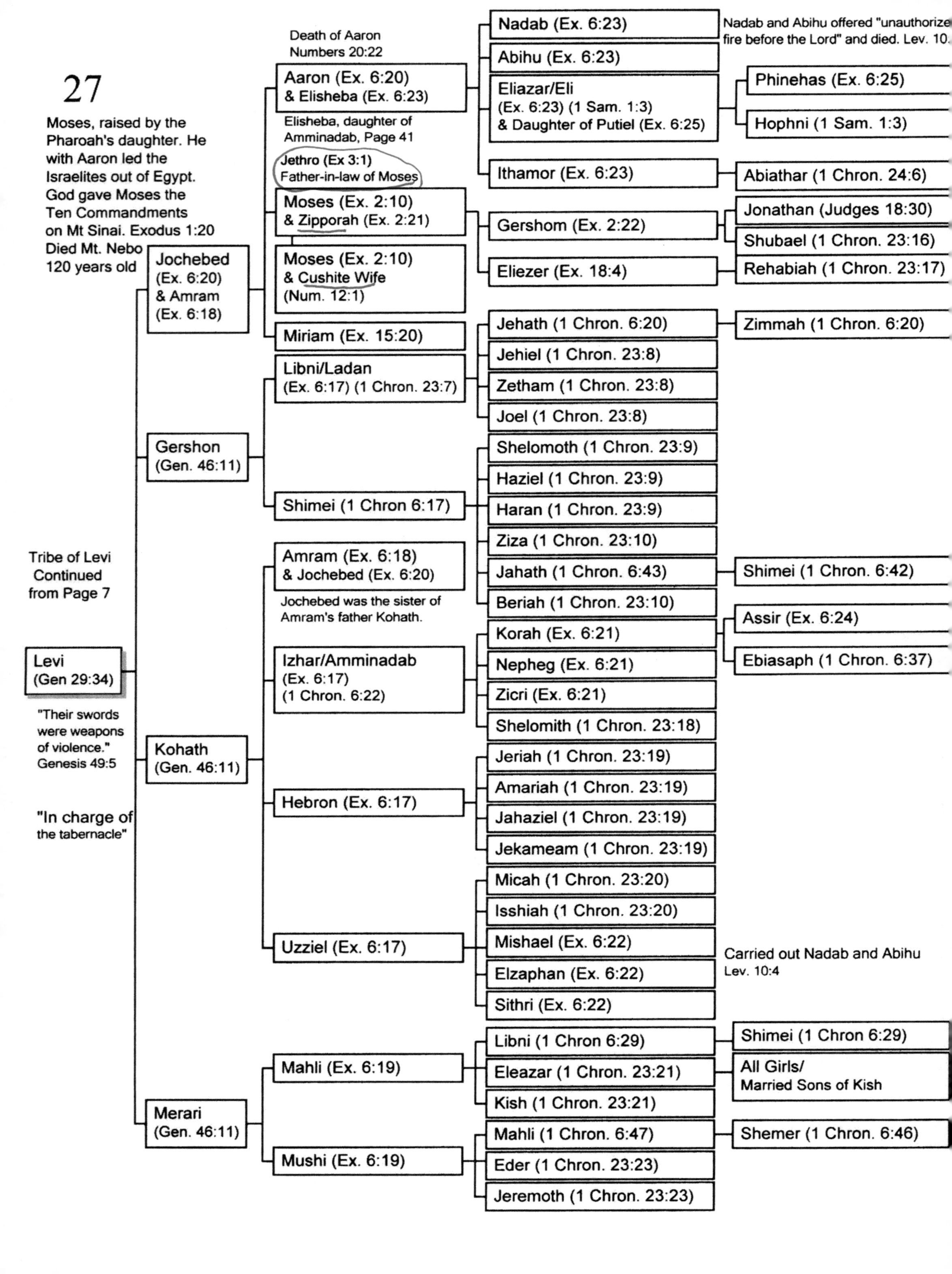
27
Moses, raised by the Pharoah's daughter. He with Aaron led the Israelites out of Egypt. God gave Moses the Ten Commandments on Mt Sinai. Exodus 1:20 Died Mt. Nebo 120 years old
Tribe of Levi Continued from Page 7
Levi (Gen 29:34)
"Their swords were weapons of violence." Genesis 49:5
"In charge of the tabernacle"
Jochebed (Ex. 6:20) & Amram (Ex. 6:18)
Gershon (Gen. 46:11)
Kohath (Gen. 46:11)
Merari (Gen. 46:11)
Death of Aaron Numbers 20:22
Aaron (Ex. 6:20) & Elisheba (Ex. 6:23)
Elisheba, daughter of Amminadab, Page 41
Jethro (Ex 3:1) Father-in-law of Moses
Moses (Ex. 2:10) & Zipporah (Ex. 2:21)
Moses (Ex. 2:10) & Cushite Wife (Num. 12:1)
Miriam (Ex. 15:20)
Libni/Ladan (Ex. 6:17) (1 Chron. 23:7)
Shimei (1 Chron 6:17)
Amram (Ex. 6:18) & Jochebed (Ex. 6:20)
Jochebed was the sister of Amram's father Kohath.
Izhar/Amminadab (Ex. 6:17) (1 Chron. 6:22)
Hebron (Ex. 6:17)
Uzziel (Ex. 6:17)
Mahli (Ex. 6:19)
Mushi (Ex. 6:19)
Nadab (Ex. 6:23)
Abihu (Ex. 6:23)
Eliazar/Eli (Ex. 6:23) (1 Sam. 1:3) & Daughter of Putiel (Ex. 6:25)
Ithamor (Ex. 6:23)
Gershom (Ex. 2:22)
Eliezer (Ex. 18:4)
Jehath (1 Chron. 6:20)
Jehiel (1 Chron. 23:8)
Zetham (1 Chron. 23:8)
Joel (1 Chron. 23:8)
Shelomoth (1 Chron. 23:9)
Haziel (1 Chron. 23:9)
Haran (1 Chron. 23:9)
Ziza (1 Chron. 23:10)
Jahath (1 Chron. 6:43)
Beriah (1 Chron. 23:10)
Korah (Ex. 6:21)
Nepheg (Ex. 6:21)
Zicri (Ex. 6:21)
Shelomith (1 Chron. 23:18)
Jeriah (1 Chron. 23:19)
Amariah (1 Chron. 23:19)
Jahaziel (1 Chron. 23:19)
Jekameam (1 Chron. 23:19)
Micah (1 Chron. 23:20)
Isshiah (1 Chron. 23:20)
Mishael (Ex. 6:22)
Elzaphan (Ex. 6:22)
Sithri (Ex. 6:22)
Libni (1 Chron 6:29)
Eleazar (1 Chron. 23:21)
Kish (1 Chron. 23:21)
Mahli (1 Chron. 6:47)
Eder (1 Chron. 23:23)
Jeremoth (1 Chron. 23:23)
Nadab and Abihu offered "unauthorize fire before the Lord" and died. Lev. 10.
Phinehas (Ex. 6:25)
Hophni (1 Sam. 1:3)
Abiathar (1 Chron. 24:6)
Jonathan (Judges 18:30)
Shubael (1 Chron. 23:16)
Rehabiah (1 Chron. 23:17)
Zimmah (1 Chron. 6:20)
Shimei (1 Chron. 6:42)
Assir (Ex. 6:24)
Ebiasaph (1 Chron. 6:37)
Carried out Nadab and Abihu Lev. 10:4
Shimei (1 Chron 6:29)
All Girls/ Married Sons of Kish
Shemer (1 Chron. 6:46)

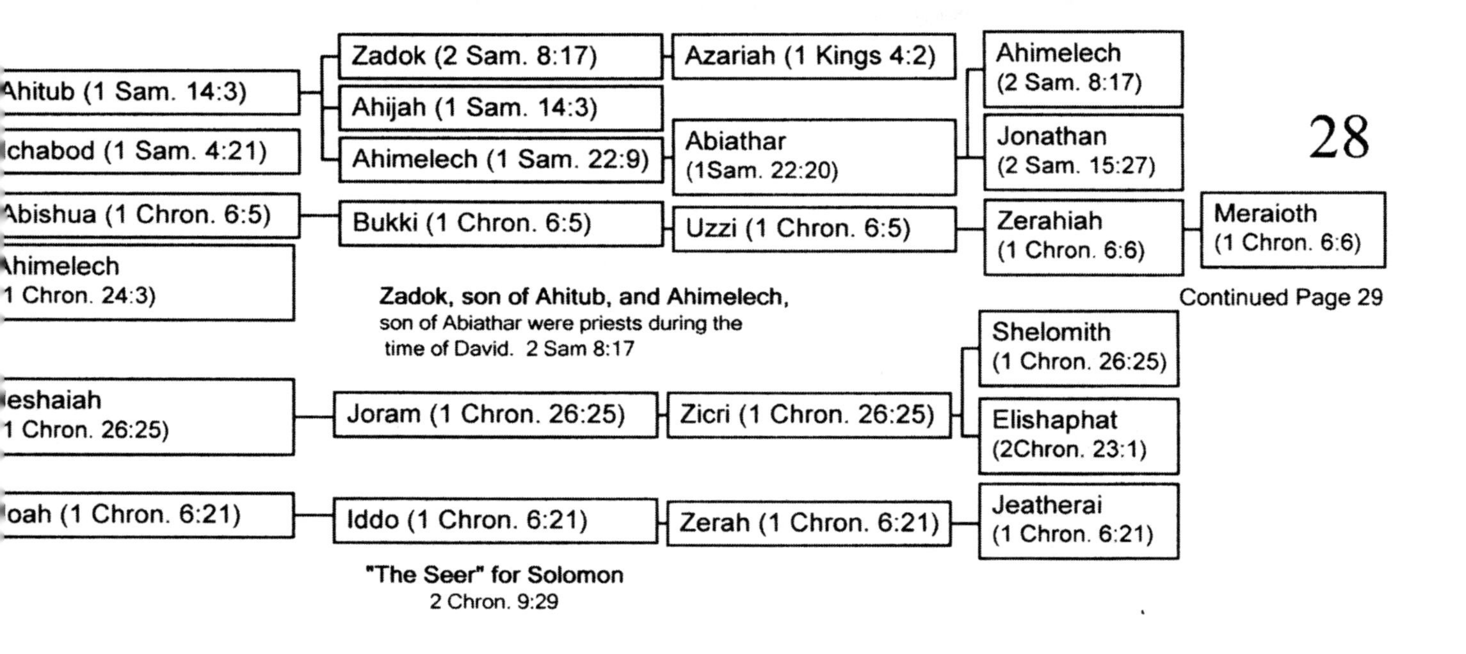

hitub (1 Sam. 14:3)
chabod (1 Sam. 4:21)
bishua (1 Chron. 6:5)
himelech
1 Chron. 24:3)
Zadok (2 Sam. 8:17)
Ahijah (1 Sam. 14:3)
Ahimelech (1 Sam. 22:9)
Bukki (1 Chron. 6:5)
Azariah (1 Kings 4:2)
Abiathar
(1Sam. 22:20)
Uzzi (1 Chron. 6:5)
Ahimelech
(2 Sam. 8:17)
Jonathan
(2 Sam. 15:27)
Zerahiah
(1 Chron. 6:6)
Meraioth
(1 Chron. 6:6)
Continued Page 29
Zadok, son of Ahitub, and Ahimelech,
son of Abiathar were priests during the
time of David. 2 Sam 8:17
eshaiah
1 Chron. 26:25)
Joram (1 Chron. 26:25)
Zicri (1 Chron. 26:25)
Shelomith
(1 Chron. 26:25)
Elishaphat
(2Chron. 23:1)
oah (1 Chron. 6:21)
Iddo (1 Chron. 6:21)
Zerah (1 Chron. 6:21)
Jeatherai
(1 Chron. 6:21)
"The Seer" for Solomon
2 Chron. 9:29

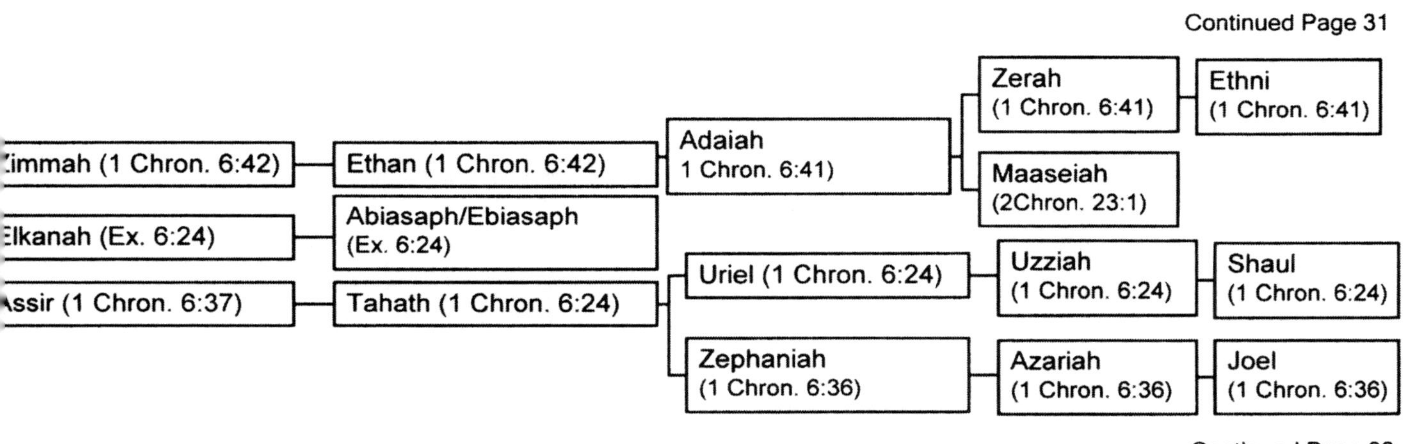

Continued Page 31
immah (1 Chron. 6:42)
lkanah (Ex. 6:24)
ssir (1 Chron. 6:37)
Ethan (1 Chron. 6:42)
Abiasaph/Ebiasaph
(Ex. 6:24)
Tahath (1 Chron. 6:24)
Adaiah
1 Chron. 6:41)
Zerah
(1 Chron. 6:41)
Ethni
(1 Chron. 6:41)
Maaseiah
(2Chron. 23:1)
Uriel (1 Chron. 6:24)
Uzziah
(1 Chron. 6:24)
Shaul
(1 Chron. 6:24)
Zephaniah
(1 Chron. 6:36)
Azariah
(1 Chron. 6:36)
Joel
(1 Chron. 6:36)
Continued Page 33

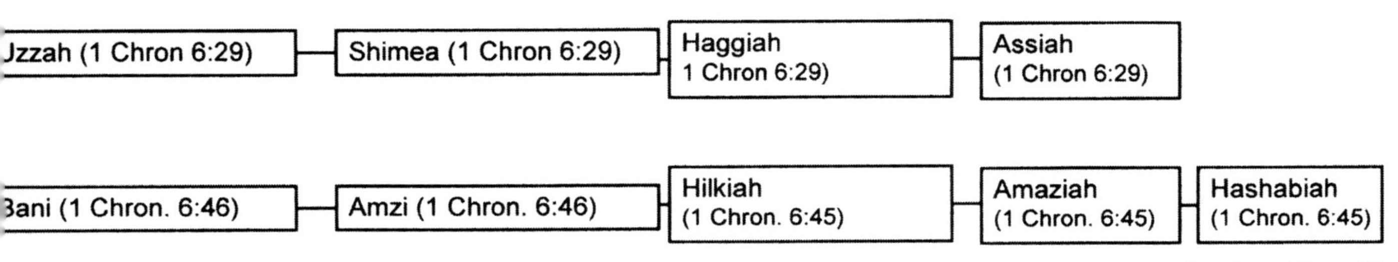

zzah (1 Chron 6:29)
Shimea (1 Chron 6:29)
Haggiah
1 Chron 6:29)
Assiah
(1 Chron 6:29)
ani (1 Chron. 6:46)
Amzi (1 Chron. 6:46)
Hilkiah
(1 Chron. 6:45)
Amaziah
(1 Chron. 6:45)
Hashabiah
(1 Chron. 6:45)
Continued Page 33

Tribe of Levi
Continued from Page 28

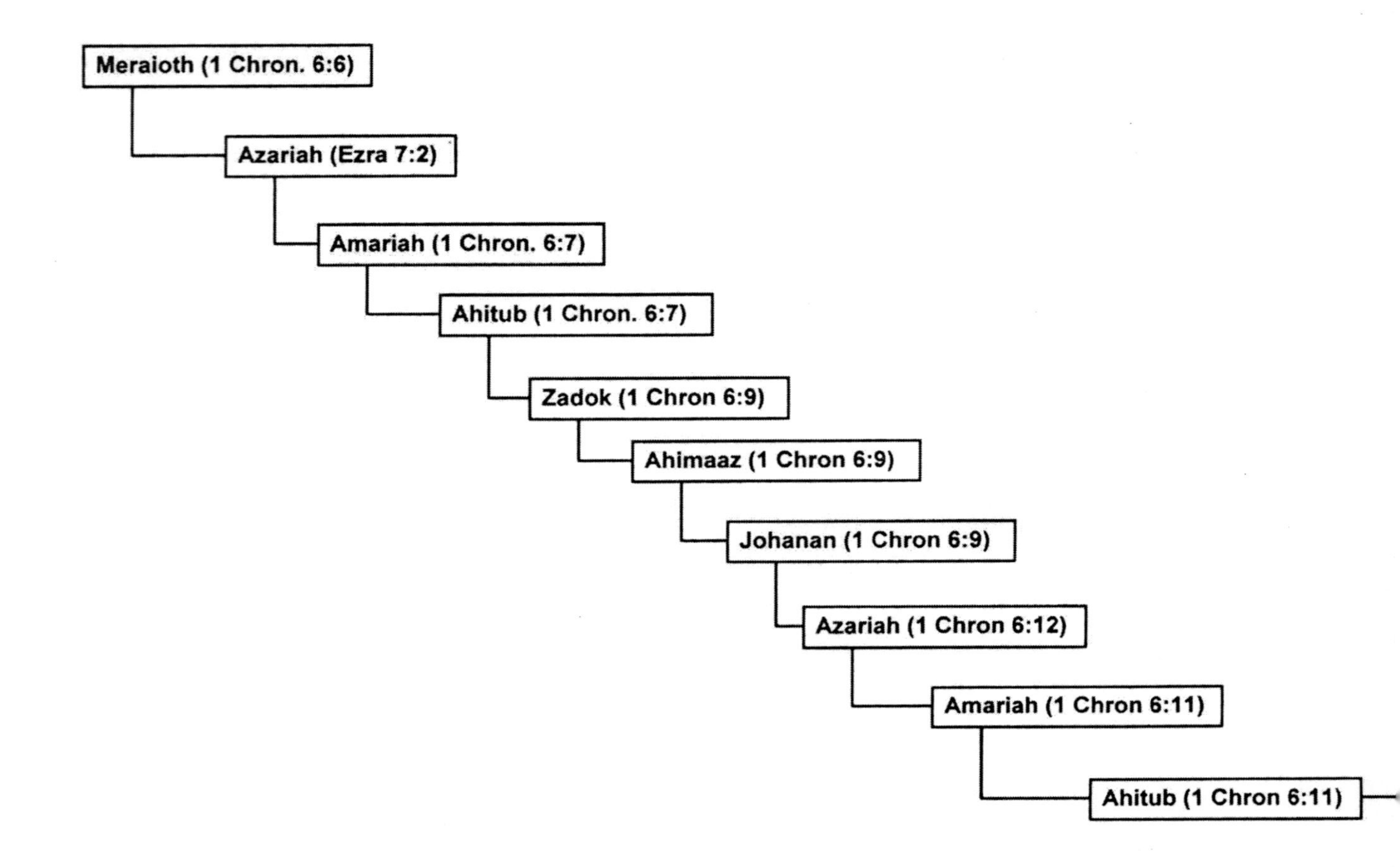
Meraioth (1 Chron. 6:6)
Azariah (Ezra 7:2)
Amariah (1 Chron. 6:7)
Ahitub (1 Chron. 6:7)
Zadok (1 Chron 6:9)
Ahimaaz (1 Chron 6:9)
Johanan (1 Chron 6:9)
Azariah (1 Chron 6:12)
Amariah (1 Chron 6:11)
Ahitub (1 Chron 6:11)

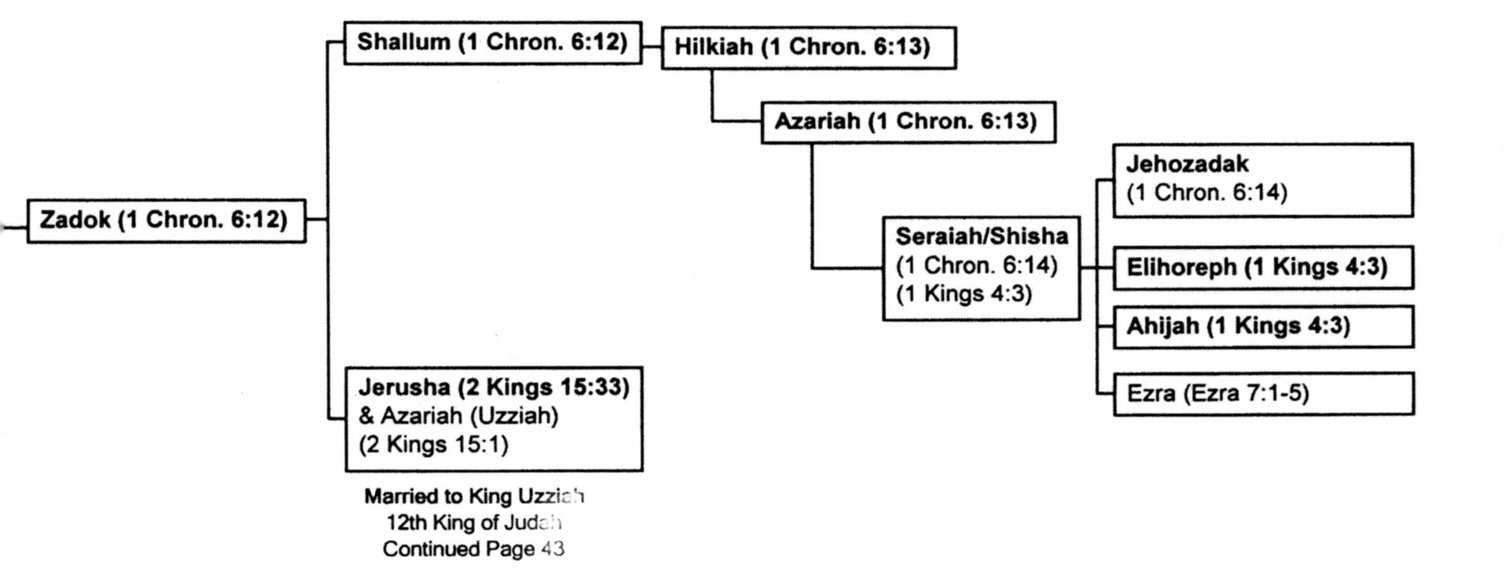
Zadok (1 Chron. 6:12)
Shallum (1 Chron. 6:12)
Hilkiah (1 Chron. 6:13)
Azariah (1 Chron. 6:13)
Seraiah/Shisha (1 Chron. 6:14) (1 Kings 4:3)
Jehozadak (1 Chron. 6:14)
Elihoreph (1 Kings 4:3)
Ahijah (1 Kings 4:3)
Ezra (Ezra 7:1-5)
Jerusha (2 Kings 15:33) & Azariah (Uzziah) (2 Kings 15:1)
Married to King Uzziah
12th King of Judah
Continued Page 43

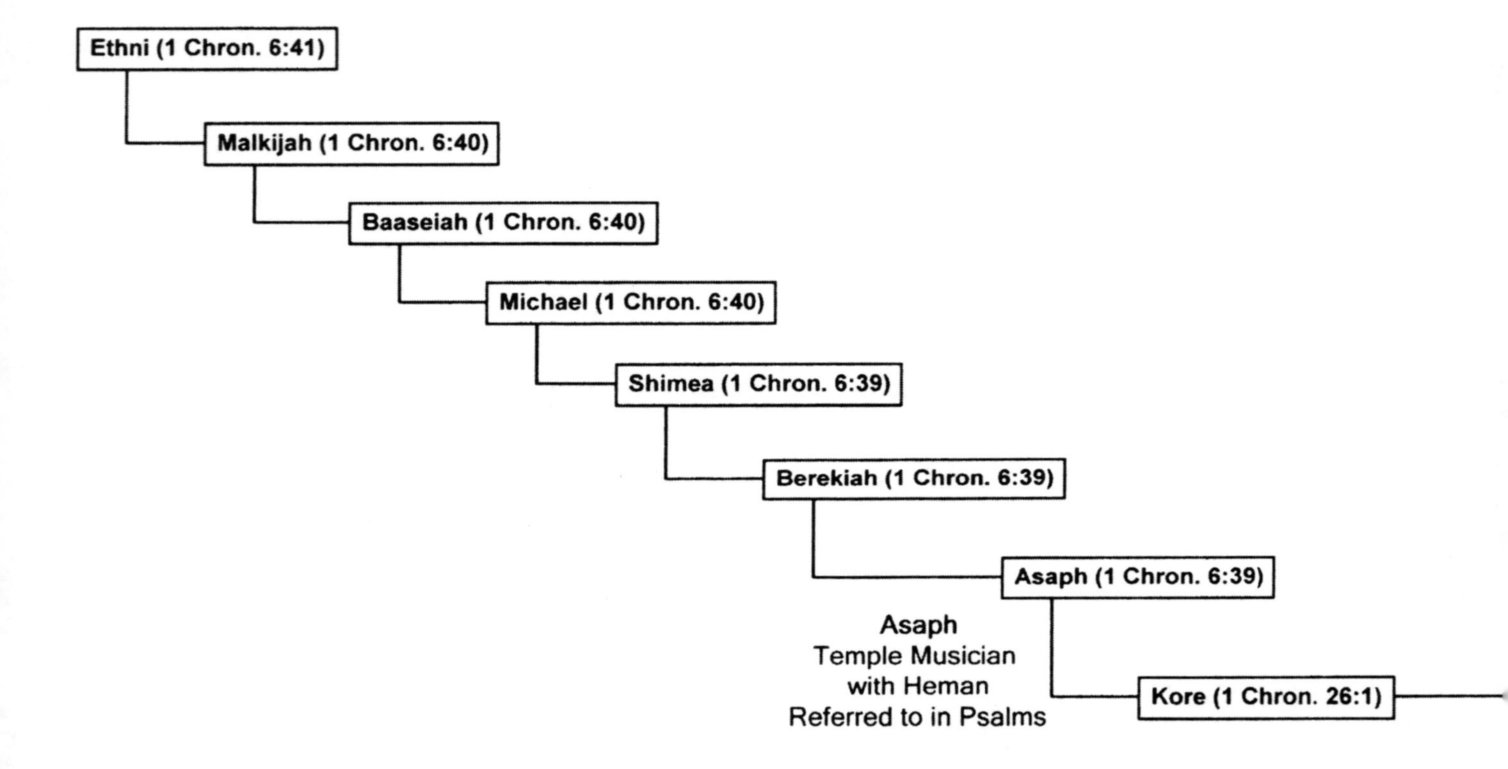
Tribe of Levi
Continued from Page 28
Ethni (1 Chron. 6:41)
Malkijah (1 Chron. 6:40)
Baaseiah (1 Chron. 6:40)
Michael (1 Chron. 6:40)
Shimea (1 Chron. 6:39)
Berekiah (1 Chron. 6:39)
Asaph (1 Chron. 6:39)
Asaph
Temple Musician
with Heman
Referred to in Psalms
Kore (1 Chron. 26:1)

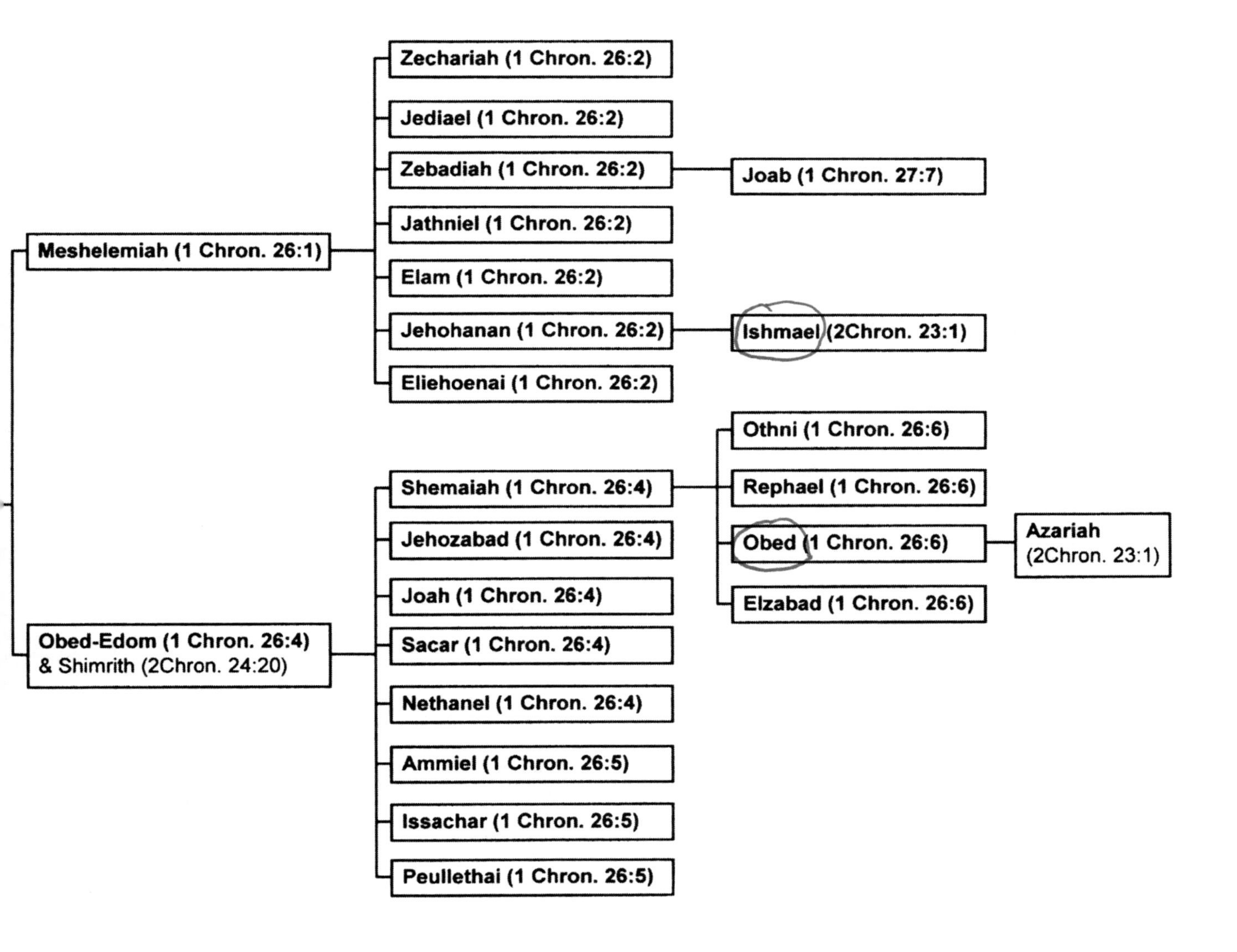
Zechariah (1 Chron. 26:2)
Jediael (1 Chron. 26:2)
Zebadiah (1 Chron. 26:2)
Joab (1 Chron. 27:7)
Jathniel (1 Chron. 26:2)
Meshelemiah (1 Chron. 26:1)
Elam (1 Chron. 26:2)
Jehohanan (1 Chron. 26:2)
Ishmael (2Chron. 23:1)
Eliehoenai (1 Chron. 26:2)
Othni (1 Chron. 26:6)
Shemaiah (1 Chron. 26:4)
Rephael (1 Chron. 26:6)
Jehozabad (1 Chron. 26:4)
Obed (1 Chron. 26:6)
Azariah
(2Chron. 23:1)
Joah (1 Chron. 26:4)
Elzabad (1 Chron. 26:6)
Obed-Edom (1 Chron. 26:4)
& Shimrith (2Chron. 24:20)
Sacar (1 Chron. 26:4)
Nethanel (1 Chron. 26:4)
Ammiel (1 Chron. 26:5)
Issachar (1 Chron. 26:5)
Peullethai (1 Chron. 26:5)

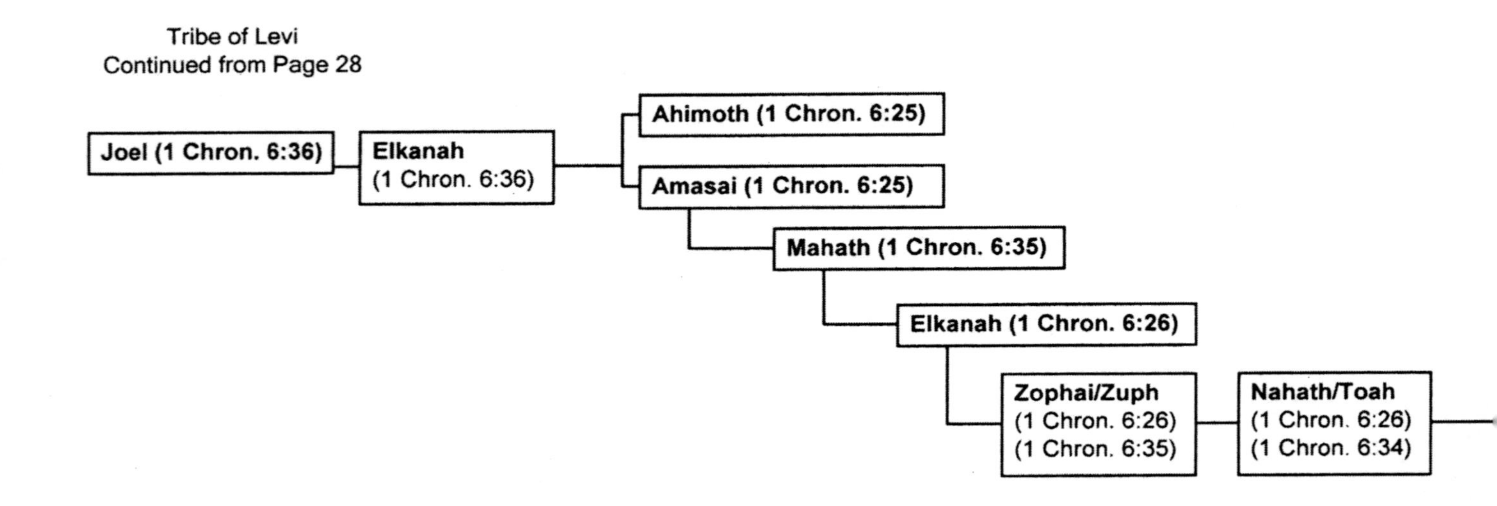
Tribe of Levi
Continued from Page 28
Joel (1 Chron. 6:36)
Elkanah
(1 Chron. 6:36)
Ahimoth (1 Chron. 6:25)
Amasai (1 Chron. 6:25)
Mahath (1 Chron. 6:35)
Elkanah (1 Chron. 6:26)
Zophai/Zuph
(1 Chron. 6:26)
(1 Chron. 6:35)
Nahath/Toah
(1 Chron. 6:26)
(1 Chron. 6:34)

Tribe of Levi

Continued from Page 28

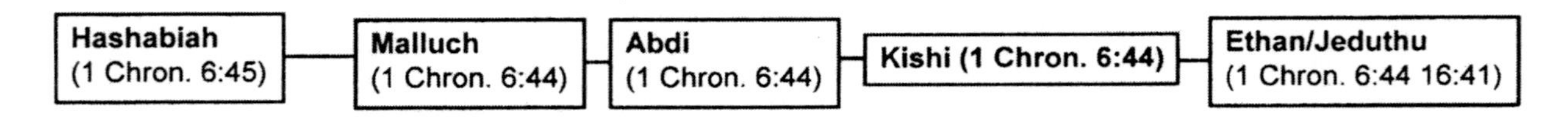
Hashabiah
(1 Chron. 6:45)
Malluch
(1 Chron. 6:44)
Abdi
(1 Chron. 6:44)
Kishi (1 Chron. 6:44)
Ethan/Jeduthu
(1 Chron. 6:44 16:41)

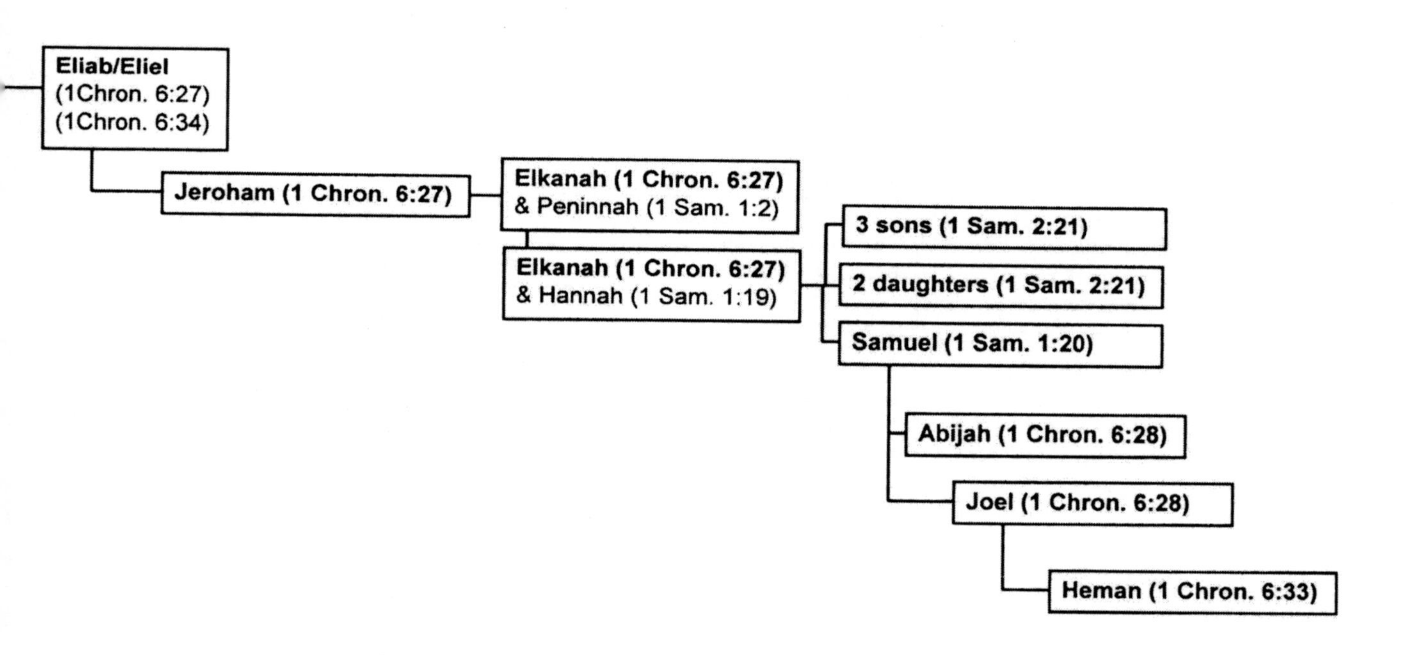

Eliab/Eliel
(1Chron. 6:27)
(1Chron. 6:34)
Jeroham (1 Chron. 6:27)
Elkanah (1 Chron. 6:27)
& Peninnah (1 Sam. 1:2)
Elkanah (1 Chron. 6:27)
& Hannah (1 Sam. 1:19)
3 sons (1 Sam. 2:21)
2 daughters (1 Sam. 2:21)
Samuel (1 Sam. 1:20)
Abijah (1 Chron. 6:28)
Joel (1 Chron. 6:28)
Heman (1 Chron. 6:33)

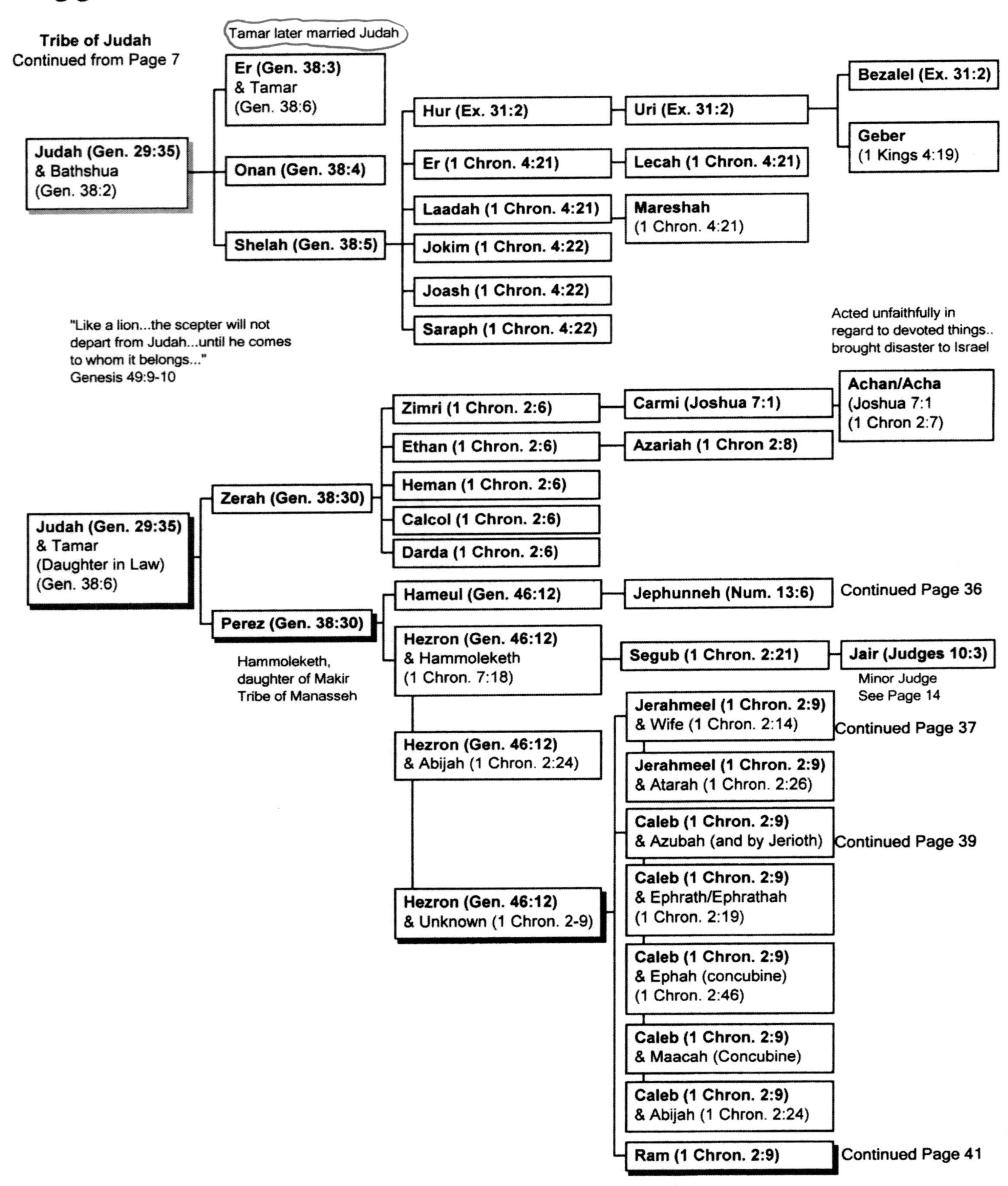
Tribe of Judah
Continued from Page 7
Tamar later married Judah
Judah (Gen. 29:35) & Bathshua (Gen. 38:2)
Er (Gen. 38:3) & Tamar (Gen. 38:6)
Onan (Gen. 38:4)
Shelah (Gen. 38:5)
Hur (Ex. 31:2)
Er (1 Chron. 4:21)
Laadah (1 Chron. 4:21)
Jokim (1 Chron. 4:22)
Joash (1 Chron. 4:22)
Saraph (1 Chron. 4:22)
Uri (Ex. 31:2)
Lecah (1 Chron. 4:21)
Mareshah (1 Chron. 4:21)
Bezalel (Ex. 31:2)
Geber (1 Kings 4:19)
"Like a lion...the scepter will not depart from Judah...until he comes to whom it belongs..." Genesis 49:9-10
Acted unfaithfully in regard to devoted things.. brought disaster to Israel
Judah (Gen. 29:35) & Tamar (Daughter in Law) (Gen. 38:6)
Zerah (Gen. 38:30)
Perez (Gen. 38:30)
Hammoleketh, daughter of Makir Tribe of Manasseh
Zimri (1 Chron. 2:6)
Ethan (1 Chron. 2:6)
Heman (1 Chron. 2:6)
Calcol (1 Chron. 2:6)
Darda (1 Chron. 2:6)
Carmi (Joshua 7:1)
Azariah (1 Chron 2:8)
Achan/Acha (Joshua 7:1 (1 Chron 2:7)
Hameul (Gen. 46:12)
Jephunneh (Num. 13:6)
Continued Page 36
Hezron (Gen. 46:12) & Hammoleketh (1 Chron. 7:18)
Segub (1 Chron. 2:21)
Jair (Judges 10:3)
Minor Judge See Page 14
Hezron (Gen. 46:12) & Abijah (1 Chron. 2:24)
Hezron (Gen. 46:12) & Unknown (1 Chron. 2-9)
Jerahmeel (1 Chron. 2:9) & Wife (1 Chron. 2:14)
Continued Page 37
Jerahmeel (1 Chron. 2:9) & Atarah (1 Chron. 2:26)
Caleb (1 Chron. 2:9) & Azubah (and by Jerioth)
Continued Page 39
Caleb (1 Chron. 2:9) & Ephrath/Ephrathah (1 Chron. 2:19)
Caleb (1 Chron. 2:9) & Ephah (concubine) (1 Chron. 2:46)
Caleb (1 Chron. 2:9) & Maacah (Concubine)
Caleb (1 Chron. 2:9) & Abijah (1 Chron. 2:24)
Ram (1 Chron. 2:9)
Continued Page 41

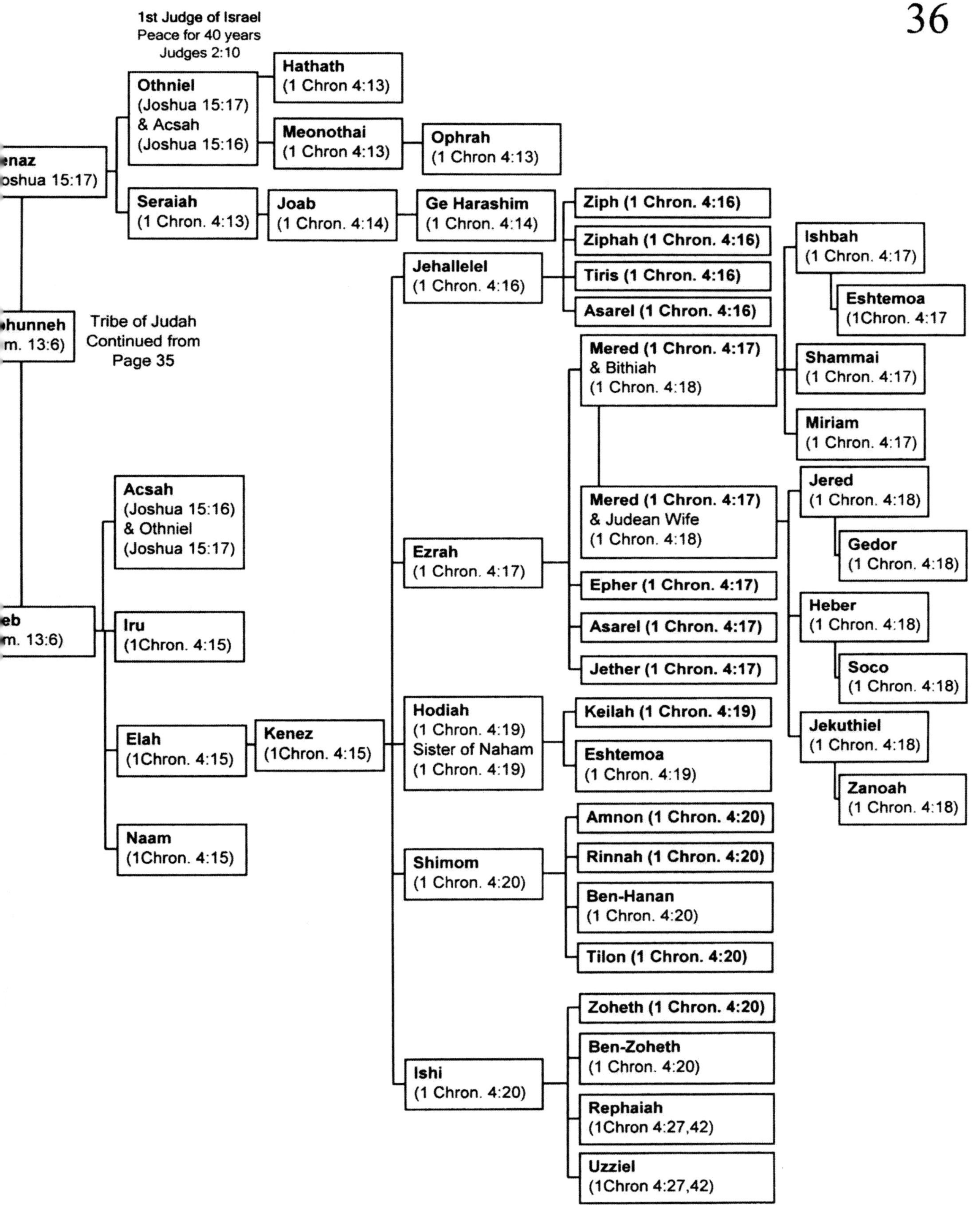
1st Judge of Israel
Peace for 40 years
Judges 2:10
Othniel (Joshua 15:17) & Acsah (Joshua 15:16)
Hathath (1 Chron 4:13)
Meonothai (1 Chron 4:13)
Ophrah (1 Chron 4:13)
enaz
oshua 15:17)
Seraiah (1 Chron. 4:13)
Joab (1 Chron. 4:14)
Ge Harashim (1 Chron. 4:14)
Ziph (1 Chron. 4:16)
Ziphah (1 Chron. 4:16)
Tiris (1 Chron. 4:16)
Asarel (1 Chron. 4:16)
Jehallelel (1 Chron. 4:16)
Ishbah (1 Chron. 4:17)
Eshtemoa (1Chron. 4:17
hunneh
m. 13:6)
Tribe of Judah
Continued from
Page 35
Mered (1 Chron. 4:17) & Bithiah (1 Chron. 4:18)
Shammai (1 Chron. 4:17)
Miriam (1 Chron. 4:17)
Mered (1 Chron. 4:17) & Judean Wife (1 Chron. 4:18)
Jered (1 Chron. 4:18)
Gedor (1 Chron. 4:18)
Acsah (Joshua 15:16) & Othniel (Joshua 15:17)
Ezrah (1 Chron. 4:17)
Epher (1 Chron. 4:17)
Asarel (1 Chron. 4:17)
Jether (1 Chron. 4:17)
Heber (1 Chron. 4:18)
Soco (1 Chron. 4:18)
eb
m. 13:6)
Iru (1Chron. 4:15)
Elah (1Chron. 4:15)
Kenez (1Chron. 4:15)
Hodiah (1 Chron. 4:19) Sister of Naham (1 Chron. 4:19)
Keilah (1 Chron. 4:19)
Eshtemoa (1 Chron. 4:19)
Jekuthiel (1 Chron. 4:18)
Zanoah (1 Chron. 4:18)
Naam (1Chron. 4:15)
Shimom (1 Chron. 4:20)
Amnon (1 Chron. 4:20)
Rinnah (1 Chron. 4:20)
Ben-Hanan (1 Chron. 4:20)
Tilon (1 Chron. 4:20)
Ishi (1 Chron. 4:20)
Zoheth (1 Chron. 4:20)
Ben-Zoheth (1 Chron. 4:20)
Rephaiah (1Chron 4:27,42)
Uzziel (1Chron 4:27,42)

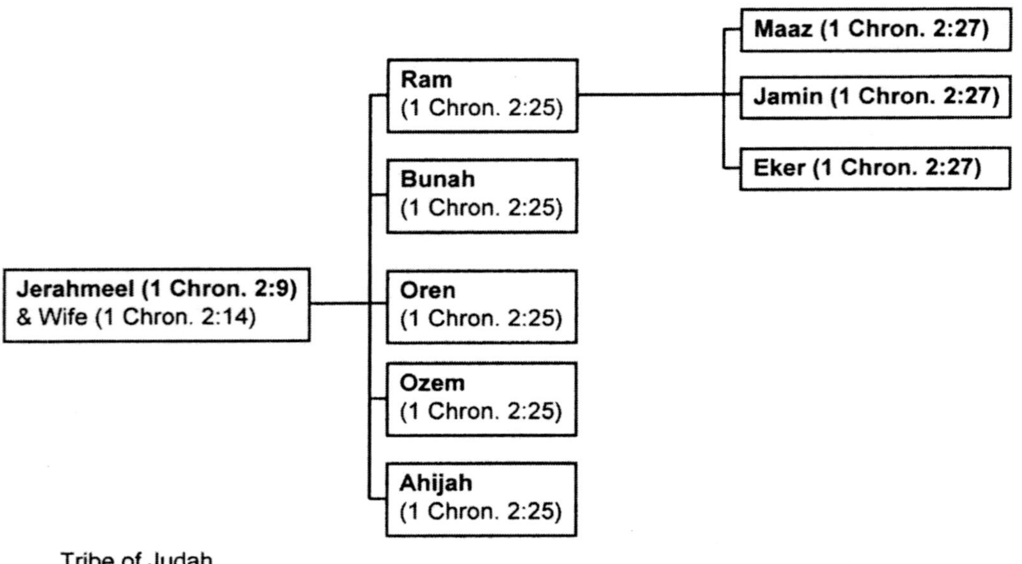
Maaz (1 Chron. 2:27)
Ram
(1 Chron. 2:25)
Jamin (1 Chron. 2:27)
Eker (1 Chron. 2:27)
Bunah
(1 Chron. 2:25)
Jerahmeel (1 Chron. 2:9)
& Wife (1 Chron. 2:14)
Oren
(1 Chron. 2:25)
Ozem
(1 Chron. 2:25)
Ahijah
(1 Chron. 2:25)

Tribe of Judah
Continued from Page 35

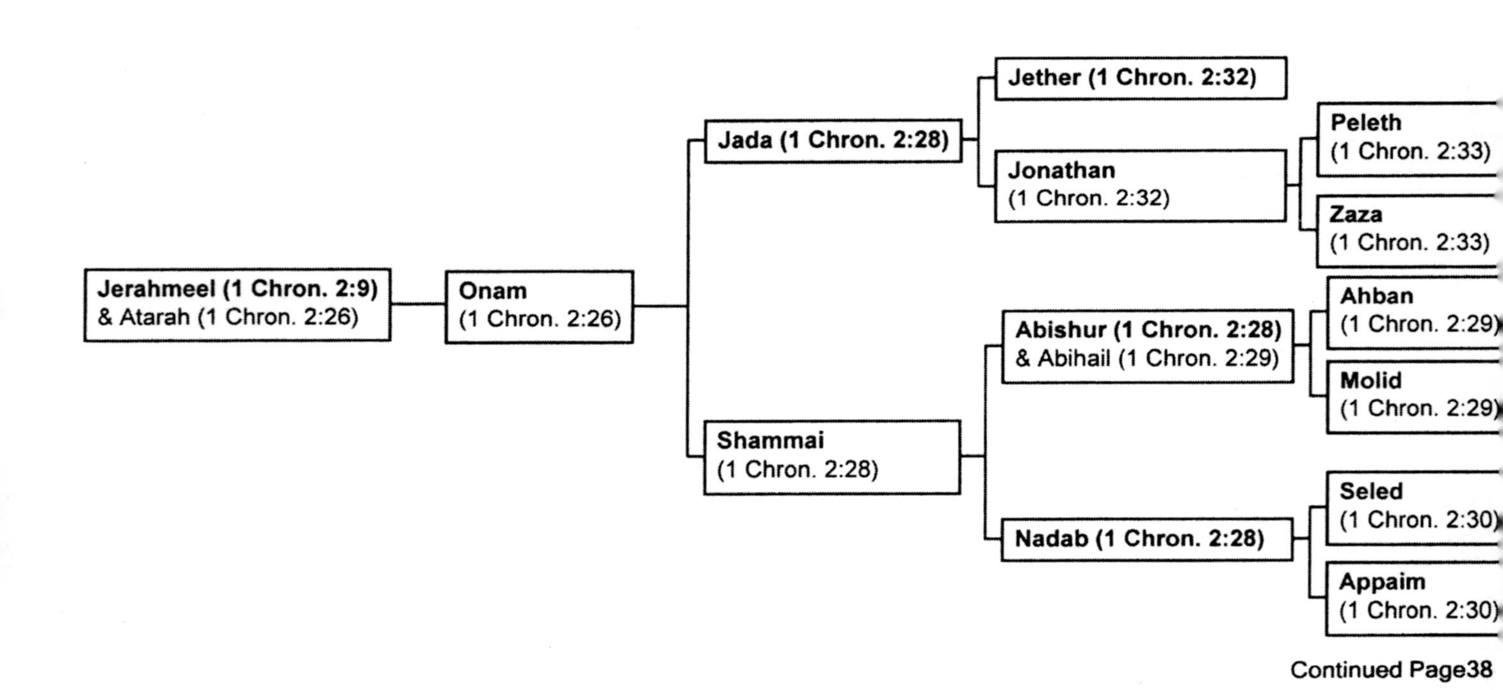
Jether (1 Chron. 2:32)
Jada (1 Chron. 2:28)
Peleth
(1 Chron. 2:33)
Jonathan
(1 Chron. 2:32)
Zaza
(1 Chron. 2:33)
Jerahmeel (1 Chron. 2:9)
& Atarah (1 Chron. 2:26)
Onam
(1 Chron. 2:26)
Ahban
(1 Chron. 2:29)
Abishur (1 Chron. 2:28)
& Abihail (1 Chron. 2:29)
Molid
(1 Chron. 2:29)
Shammai
(1 Chron. 2:28)
Seled
(1 Chron. 2:30)
Nadab (1 Chron. 2:28)
Appaim
(1 Chron. 2:30)

Continued Page38

Tribe of Judah
Continued from Page 37

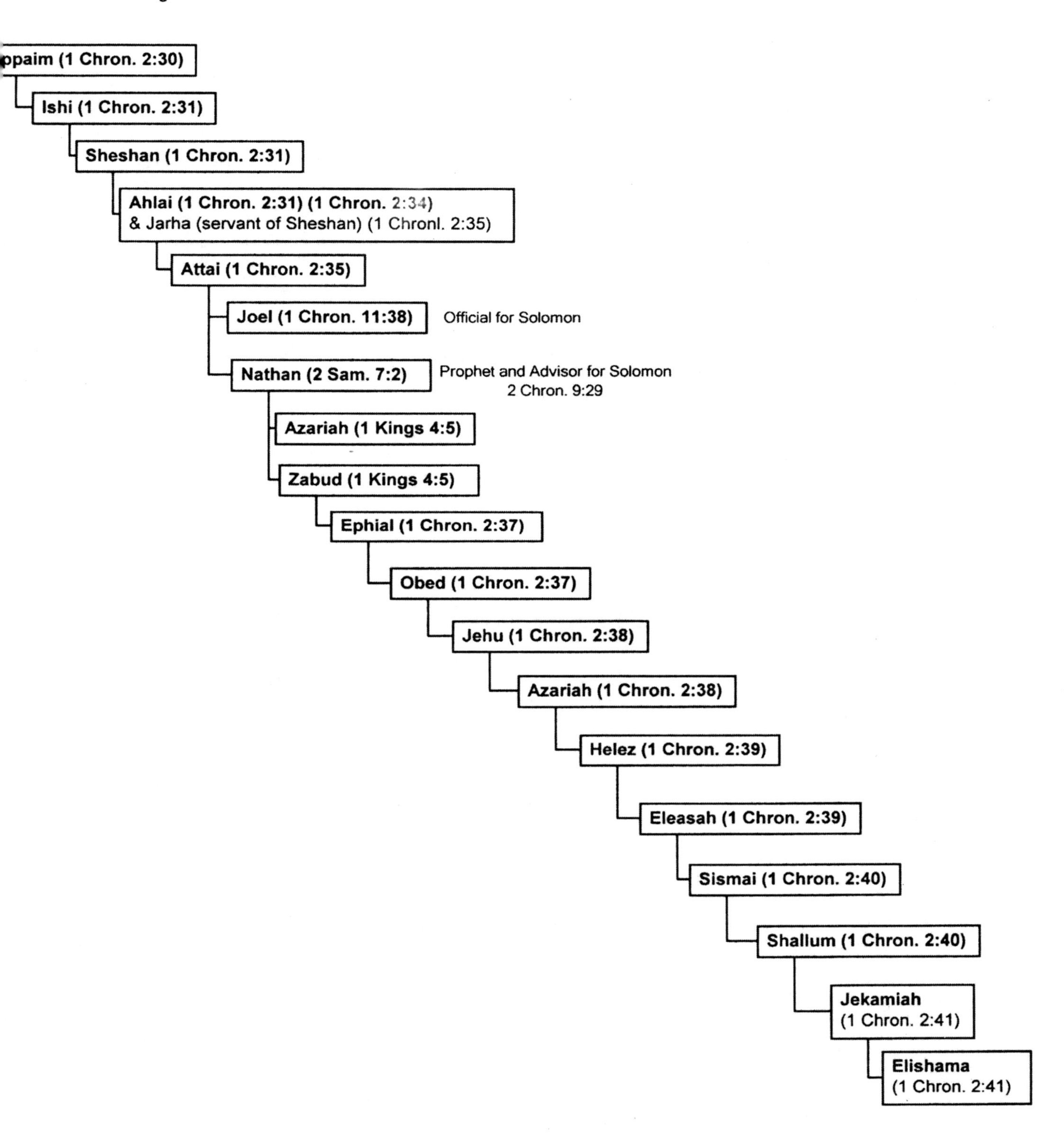
ppaim (1 Chron. 2:30)
Ishi (1 Chron. 2:31)
Sheshan (1 Chron. 2:31)
Ahlai (1 Chron. 2:31) (1 Chron. 2:34)
& Jarha (servant of Sheshan) (1 Chronl. 2:35)
Attai (1 Chron. 2:35)
Joel (1 Chron. 11:38)
Official for Solomon
Nathan (2 Sam. 7:2)
Prophet and Advisor for Solomon
2 Chron. 9:29
Azariah (1 Kings 4:5)
Zabud (1 Kings 4:5)
Ephial (1 Chron. 2:37)
Obed (1 Chron. 2:37)
Jehu (1 Chron. 2:38)
Azariah (1 Chron. 2:38)
Helez (1 Chron. 2:39)
Eleasah (1 Chron. 2:39)
Sismai (1 Chron. 2:40)
Shallum (1 Chron. 2:40)
Jekamiah
(1 Chron. 2:41)
Elishama
(1 Chron. 2:41)

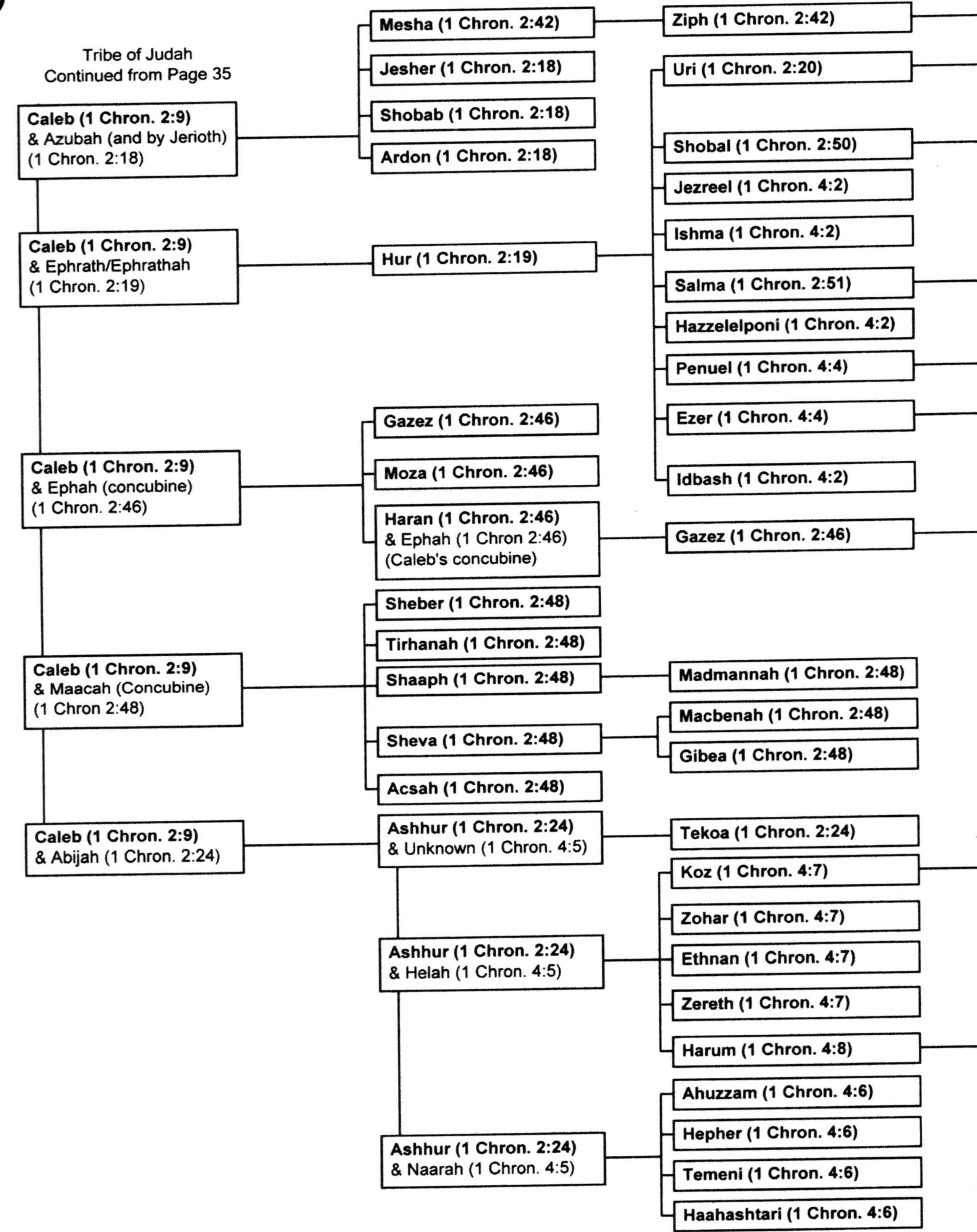
Tribe of Judah
Continued from Page 35
Caleb (1 Chron. 2:9)
& Azubah (and by Jerioth)
(1 Chron. 2:18)
Mesha (1 Chron. 2:42)
Jesher (1 Chron. 2:18)
Shobab (1 Chron. 2:18)
Ardon (1 Chron. 2:18)
Ziph (1 Chron. 2:42)
Caleb (1 Chron. 2:9)
& Ephrath/Ephrathah
(1 Chron. 2:19)
Hur (1 Chron. 2:19)
Uri (1 Chron. 2:20)
Shobal (1 Chron. 2:50)
Jezreel (1 Chron. 4:2)
Ishma (1 Chron. 4:2)
Salma (1 Chron. 2:51)
Hazzelelponi (1 Chron. 4:2)
Penuel (1 Chron. 4:4)
Ezer (1 Chron. 4:4)
Idbash (1 Chron. 4:2)
Caleb (1 Chron. 2:9)
& Ephah (concubine)
(1 Chron. 2:46)
Gazez (1 Chron. 2:46)
Moza (1 Chron. 2:46)
Haran (1 Chron. 2:46)
& Ephah (1 Chron 2:46)
(Caleb's concubine)
Gazez (1 Chron. 2:46)
Caleb (1 Chron. 2:9)
& Maacah (Concubine)
(1 Chron 2:48)
Sheber (1 Chron. 2:48)
Tirhanah (1 Chron. 2:48)
Shaaph (1 Chron. 2:48)
Madmannah (1 Chron. 2:48)
Sheva (1 Chron. 2:48)
Macbenah (1 Chron. 2:48)
Gibea (1 Chron. 2:48)
Acsah (1 Chron. 2:48)
Caleb (1 Chron. 2:9)
& Abijah (1 Chron. 2:24)
Ashhur (1 Chron. 2:24)
& Unknown (1 Chron. 4:5)
Tekoa (1 Chron. 2:24)
Ashhur (1 Chron. 2:24)
& Helah (1 Chron. 4:5)
Koz (1 Chron. 4:7)
Zohar (1 Chron. 4:7)
Ethnan (1 Chron. 4:7)
Zereth (1 Chron. 4:7)
Harum (1 Chron. 4:8)
Ashhur (1 Chron. 2:24)
& Naarah (1 Chron. 4:5)
Ahuzzam (1 Chron. 4:6)
Hepher (1 Chron. 4:6)
Temeni (1 Chron. 4:6)
Haahashtari (1 Chron. 4:6)

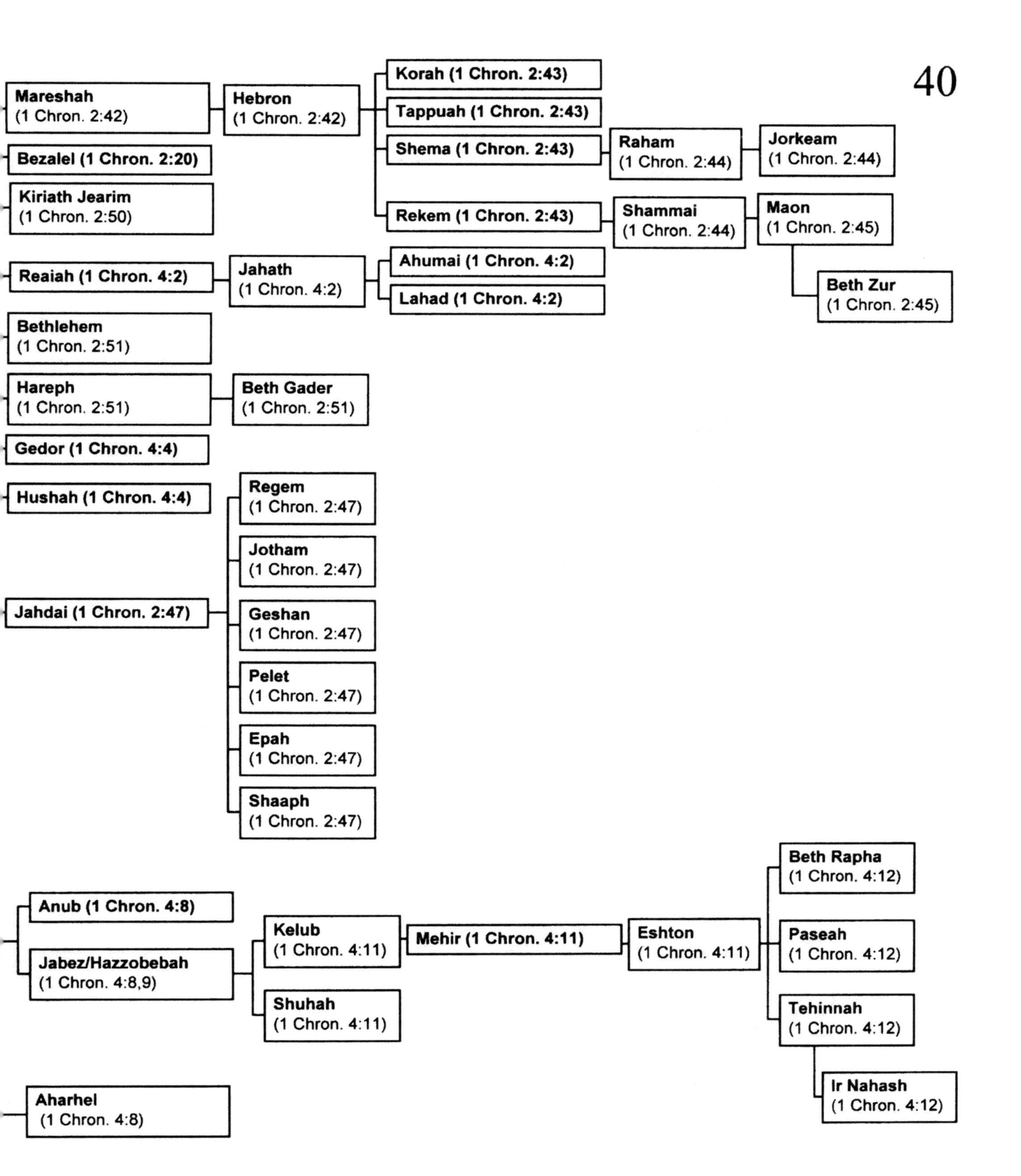
Mareshah (1 Chron. 2:42)
Hebron (1 Chron. 2:42)
Korah (1 Chron. 2:43)
Tappuah (1 Chron. 2:43)
Shema (1 Chron. 2:43)
Raham (1 Chron. 2:44)
Jorkeam (1 Chron. 2:44)
Rekem (1 Chron. 2:43)
Shammai (1 Chron. 2:44)
Maon (1 Chron. 2:45)
Beth Zur (1 Chron. 2:45)
Bezalel (1 Chron. 2:20)
Kiriath Jearim (1 Chron. 2:50)
Reaiah (1 Chron. 4:2)
Jahath (1 Chron. 4:2)
Ahumai (1 Chron. 4:2)
Lahad (1 Chron. 4:2)
Bethlehem (1 Chron. 2:51)
Hareph (1 Chron. 2:51)
Beth Gader (1 Chron. 2:51)
Gedor (1 Chron. 4:4)
Hushah (1 Chron. 4:4)
Jahdai (1 Chron. 2:47)
Regem (1 Chron. 2:47)
Jotham (1 Chron. 2:47)
Geshan (1 Chron. 2:47)
Pelet (1 Chron. 2:47)
Epah (1 Chron. 2:47)
Shaaph (1 Chron. 2:47)
Anub (1 Chron. 4:8)
Jabez/Hazzobebah (1 Chron. 4:8,9)
Kelub (1 Chron. 4:11)
Shuhah (1 Chron. 4:11)
Mehir (1 Chron. 4:11)
Eshton (1 Chron. 4:11)
Beth Rapha (1 Chron. 4:12)
Paseah (1 Chron. 4:12)
Tehinnah (1 Chron. 4:12)
Ir Nahash (1 Chron. 4:12)
Aharhel (1 Chron. 4:8)

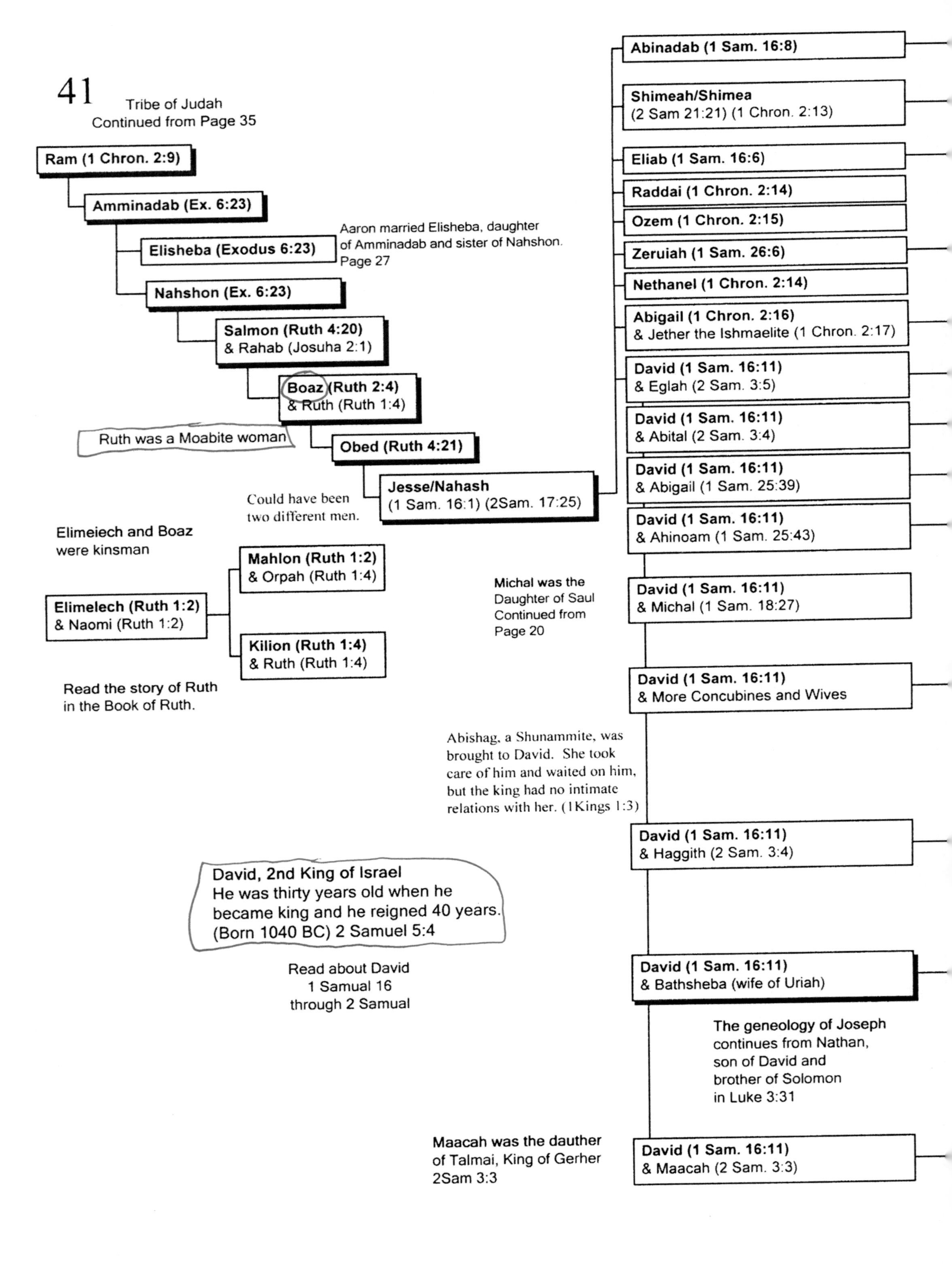

41
Tribe of Judah
Continued from Page 35
Ram (1 Chron. 2:9)
Amminadab (Ex. 6:23)
Elisheba (Exodus 6:23)
Aaron married Elisheba, daughter of Amminadab and sister of Nahshon. Page 27
Nahshon (Ex. 6:23)
Salmon (Ruth 4:20) & Rahab (Josuha 2:1)
Boaz (Ruth 2:4) & Ruth (Ruth 1:4)
Ruth was a Moabite woman
Obed (Ruth 4:21)
Jesse/Nahash (1 Sam. 16:1) (2Sam. 17:25)
Could have been two different men.
Elimeiech and Boaz were kinsman
Mahlon (Ruth 1:2) & Orpah (Ruth 1:4)
Elimelech (Ruth 1:2) & Naomi (Ruth 1:2)
Kilion (Ruth 1:4) & Ruth (Ruth 1:4)
Read the story of Ruth in the Book of Ruth.
Abinadab (1 Sam. 16:8)
Shimeah/Shimea (2 Sam 21:21) (1 Chron. 2:13)
Eliab (1 Sam. 16:6)
Raddai (1 Chron. 2:14)
Ozem (1 Chron. 2:15)
Zeruiah (1 Sam. 26:6)
Nethanel (1 Chron. 2:14)
Abigail (1 Chron. 2:16) & Jether the Ishmaelite (1 Chron. 2:17)
David (1 Sam. 16:11) & Eglah (2 Sam. 3:5)
David (1 Sam. 16:11) & Abital (2 Sam. 3:4)
David (1 Sam. 16:11) & Abigail (1 Sam. 25:39)
David (1 Sam. 16:11) & Ahinoam (1 Sam. 25:43)
Michal was the Daughter of Saul Continued from Page 20
David (1 Sam. 16:11) & Michal (1 Sam. 18:27)
David (1 Sam. 16:11) & More Concubines and Wives
Abishag, a Shunammite, was brought to David. She took care of him and waited on him, but the king had no intimate relations with her. (1Kings 1:3)
David (1 Sam. 16:11) & Haggith (2 Sam. 3:4)
David, 2nd King of Israel
He was thirty years old when he became king and he reigned 40 years. (Born 1040 BC) 2 Samuel 5:4
Read about David 1 Samual 16 through 2 Samual
David (1 Sam. 16:11) & Bathsheba (wife of Uriah)
The geneology of Joseph continues from Nathan, son of David and brother of Solomon in Luke 3:31
Maacah was the dauther of Talmai, King of Gerher 2Sam 3:3
David (1 Sam. 16:11) & Maacah (2 Sam. 3:3)

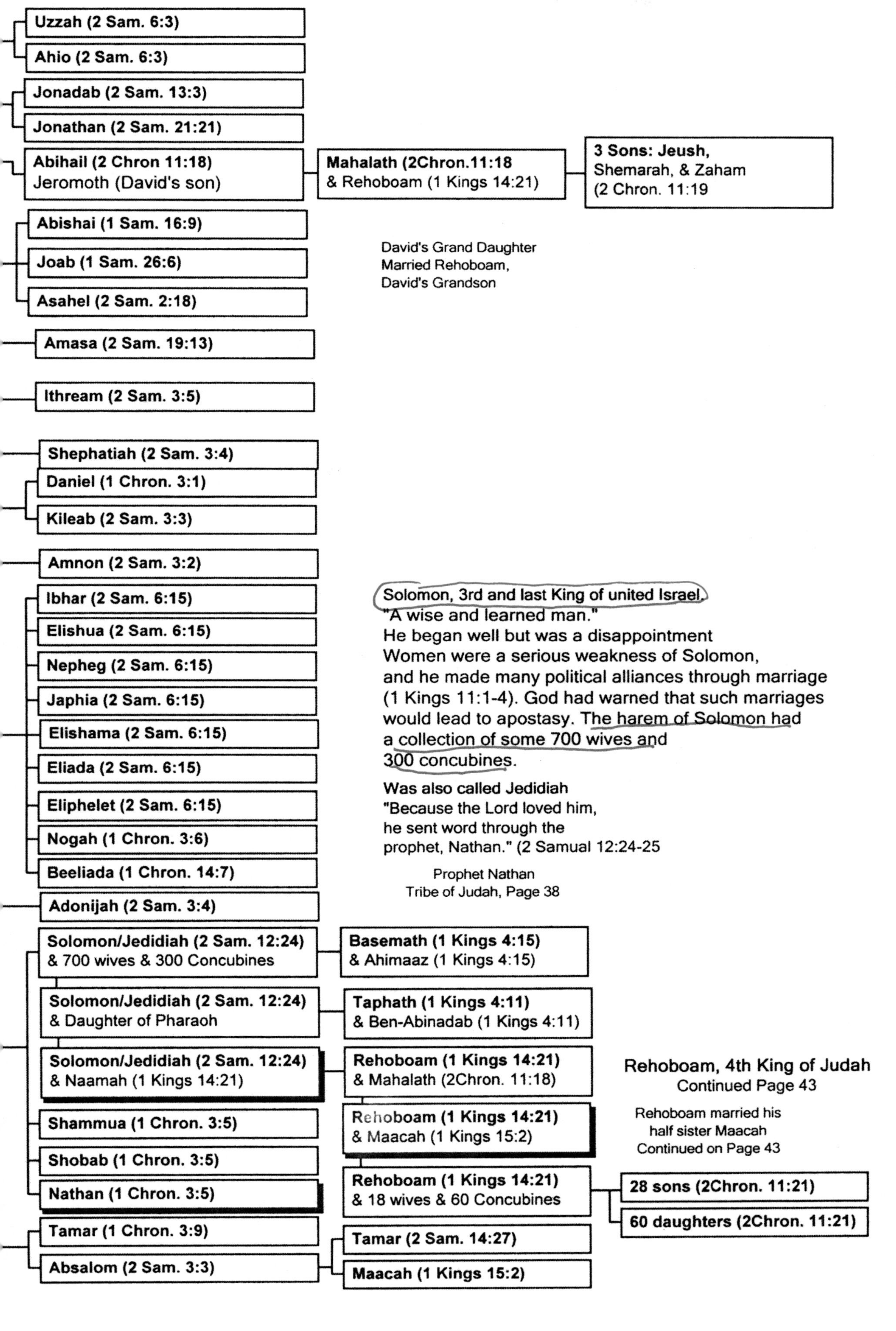
Uzzah (2 Sam. 6:3)
Ahio (2 Sam. 6:3)
Jonadab (2 Sam. 13:3)
Jonathan (2 Sam. 21:21)
Abihail (2 Chron 11:18)
Jeromoth (David's son)
Mahalath (2Chron.11:18
& Rehoboam (1 Kings 14:21)
3 Sons: Jeush,
Shemarah, & Zaham
(2 Chron. 11:19
Abishai (1 Sam. 16:9)
Joab (1 Sam. 26:6)
Asahel (2 Sam. 2:18)
David's Grand Daughter
Married Rehoboam,
David's Grandson
Amasa (2 Sam. 19:13)
Ithream (2 Sam. 3:5)
Shephatiah (2 Sam. 3:4)
Daniel (1 Chron. 3:1)
Kileab (2 Sam. 3:3)
Amnon (2 Sam. 3:2)
Ibhar (2 Sam. 6:15)
Elishua (2 Sam. 6:15)
Nepheg (2 Sam. 6:15)
Japhia (2 Sam. 6:15)
Elishama (2 Sam. 6:15)
Eliada (2 Sam. 6:15)
Eliphelet (2 Sam. 6:15)
Nogah (1 Chron. 3:6)
Beeliada (1 Chron. 14:7)
Solomon, 3rd and last King of united Israel.
"A wise and learned man."
He began well but was a disappointment
Women were a serious weakness of Solomon,
and he made many political alliances through marriage
(1 Kings 11:1-4). God had warned that such marriages
would lead to apostasy. The harem of Solomon had
a collection of some 700 wives and
300 concubines.
Was also called Jedidiah
"Because the Lord loved him,
he sent word through the
prophet, Nathan." (2 Samual 12:24-25
Prophet Nathan
Tribe of Judah, Page 38
Adonijah (2 Sam. 3:4)
Solomon/Jedidiah (2 Sam. 12:24)
& 700 wives & 300 Concubines
Basemath (1 Kings 4:15)
& Ahimaaz (1 Kings 4:15)
Solomon/Jedidiah (2 Sam. 12:24)
& Daughter of Pharaoh
Taphath (1 Kings 4:11)
& Ben-Abinadab (1 Kings 4:11)
Solomon/Jedidiah (2 Sam. 12:24)
& Naamah (1 Kings 14:21)
Rehoboam (1 Kings 14:21)
& Mahalath (2Chron. 11:18)
Rehoboam, 4th King of Judah
Continued Page 43
Shammua (1 Chron. 3:5)
Rehoboam (1 Kings 14:21)
& Maacah (1 Kings 15:2)
Rehoboam married his
half sister Maacah
Continued on Page 43
Shobab (1 Chron. 3:5)
Nathan (1 Chron. 3:5)
Rehoboam (1 Kings 14:21)
& 18 wives & 60 Concubines
28 sons (2Chron. 11:21)
60 daughters (2Chron. 11:21)
Tamar (1 Chron. 3:9)
Absalom (2 Sam. 3:3)
Tamar (2 Sam. 14:27)
Maacah (1 Kings 15:2)

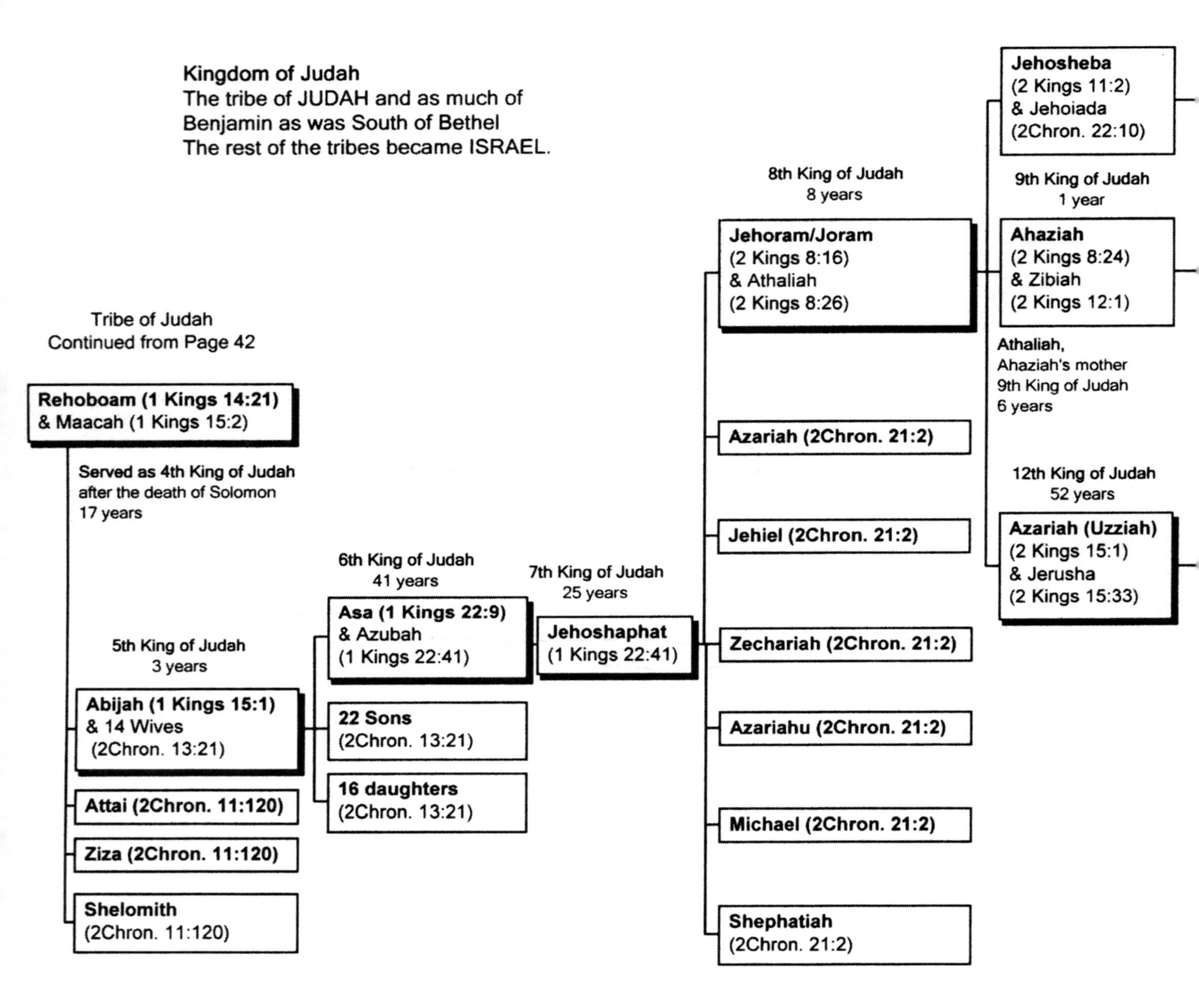

Kingdom of Judah
The tribe of JUDAH and as much of
Benjamin as was South of Bethel
The rest of the tribes became ISRAEL.
Tribe of Judah
Continued from Page 42
Rehoboam (1 Kings 14:21)
& Maacah (1 Kings 15:2)
Served as 4th King of Judah
after the death of Solomon
17 years
5th King of Judah
3 years
Abijah (1 Kings 15:1)
& 14 Wives
(2Chron. 13:21)
Attai (2Chron. 11:120)
Ziza (2Chron. 11:120)
Shelomith
(2Chron. 11:120)
6th King of Judah
41 years
Asa (1 Kings 22:9)
& Azubah
(1 Kings 22:41)
22 Sons
(2Chron. 13:21)
16 daughters
(2Chron. 13:21)
7th King of Judah
25 years
Jehoshaphat
(1 Kings 22:41)
8th King of Judah
8 years
Jehoram/Joram
(2 Kings 8:16)
& Athaliah
(2 Kings 8:26)
Azariah (2Chron. 21:2)
Jehiel (2Chron. 21:2)
Zechariah (2Chron. 21:2)
Azariahu (2Chron. 21:2)
Michael (2Chron. 21:2)
Shephatiah
(2Chron. 21:2)
Jehosheba
(2 Kings 11:2)
& Jehoiada
(2Chron. 22:10)
9th King of Judah
1 year
Ahaziah
(2 Kings 8:24)
& Zibiah
(2 Kings 12:1)
Athaliah,
Ahaziah's mother
9th King of Judah
6 years
12th King of Judah
52 years
Azariah (Uzziah)
(2 Kings 15:1)
& Jerusha
(2 Kings 15:33)

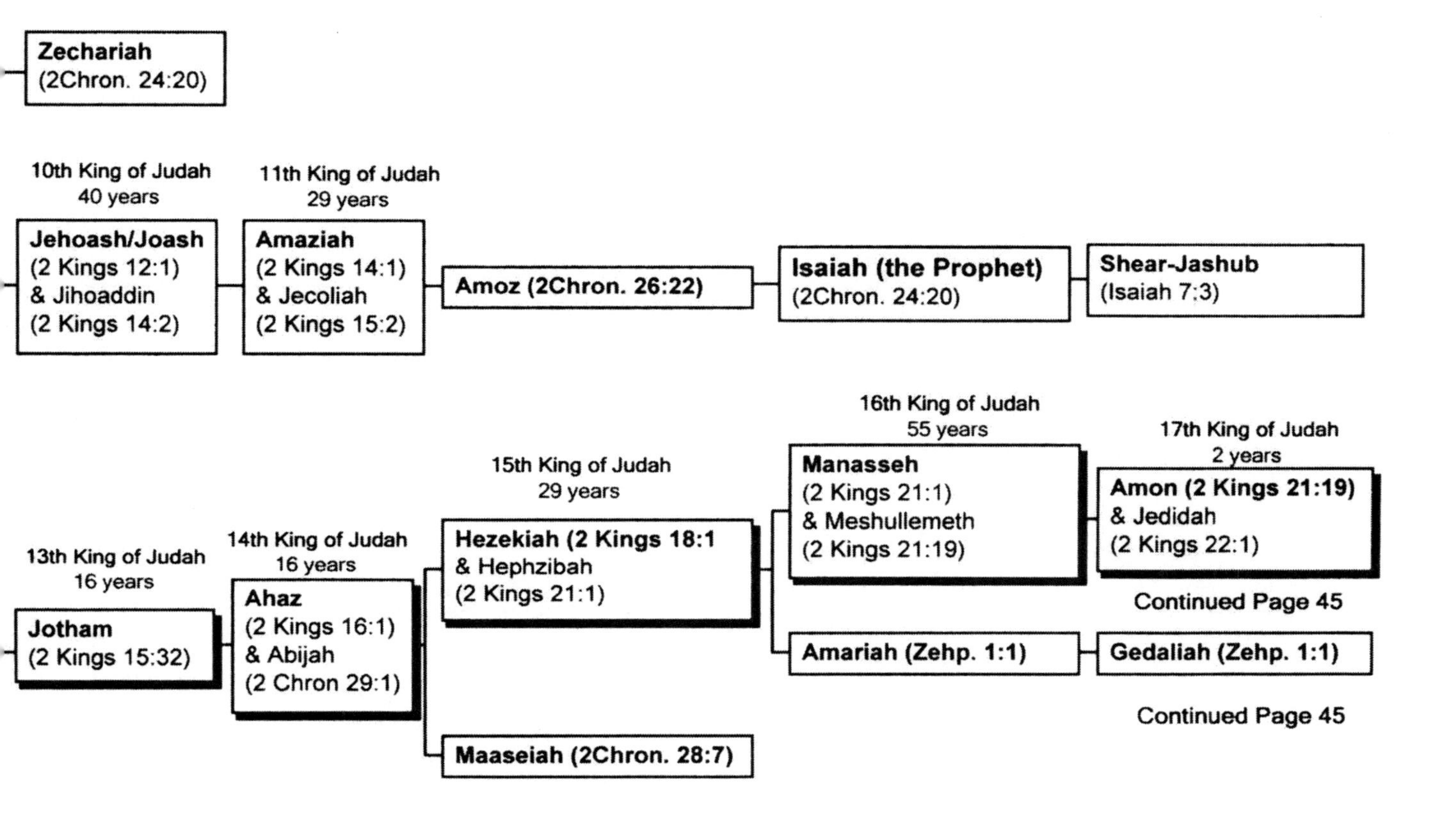
Zechariah
(2Chron. 24:20)
10th King of Judah
40 years
Jehoash/Joash
(2 Kings 12:1)
& Jihoaddin
(2 Kings 14:2)
11th King of Judah
29 years
Amaziah
(2 Kings 14:1)
& Jecoliah
(2 Kings 15:2)
Amoz (2Chron. 26:22)
Isaiah (the Prophet)
(2Chron. 24:20)
Shear-Jashub
(Isaiah 7:3)
13th King of Judah
16 years
Jotham
(2 Kings 15:32)
14th King of Judah
16 years
Ahaz
(2 Kings 16:1)
& Abijah
(2 Chron 29:1)
15th King of Judah
29 years
Hezekiah (2 Kings 18:1
& Hephzibah
(2 Kings 21:1)
Maaseiah (2Chron. 28:7)
16th King of Judah
55 years
Manasseh
(2 Kings 21:1)
& Meshullemeth
(2 Kings 21:19)
Amariah (Zehp. 1:1)
17th King of Judah
2 years
Amon (2 Kings 21:19)
& Jedidah
(2 Kings 22:1)
Continued Page 45
Gedaliah (Zehp. 1:1)
Continued Page 45

Of 20 Kings of Judah, all descendents of David, who for 388 years held the throne, six are mentioned with great praise--ASA, JEHOSAPHAT, UZZIAH, JOTHAM, HEZEKIAH AND JOSIAH.

Others were fearfully wicked-- JEHORAM, AHAZ, MANASSEH, AND AMON, all introduced idols.

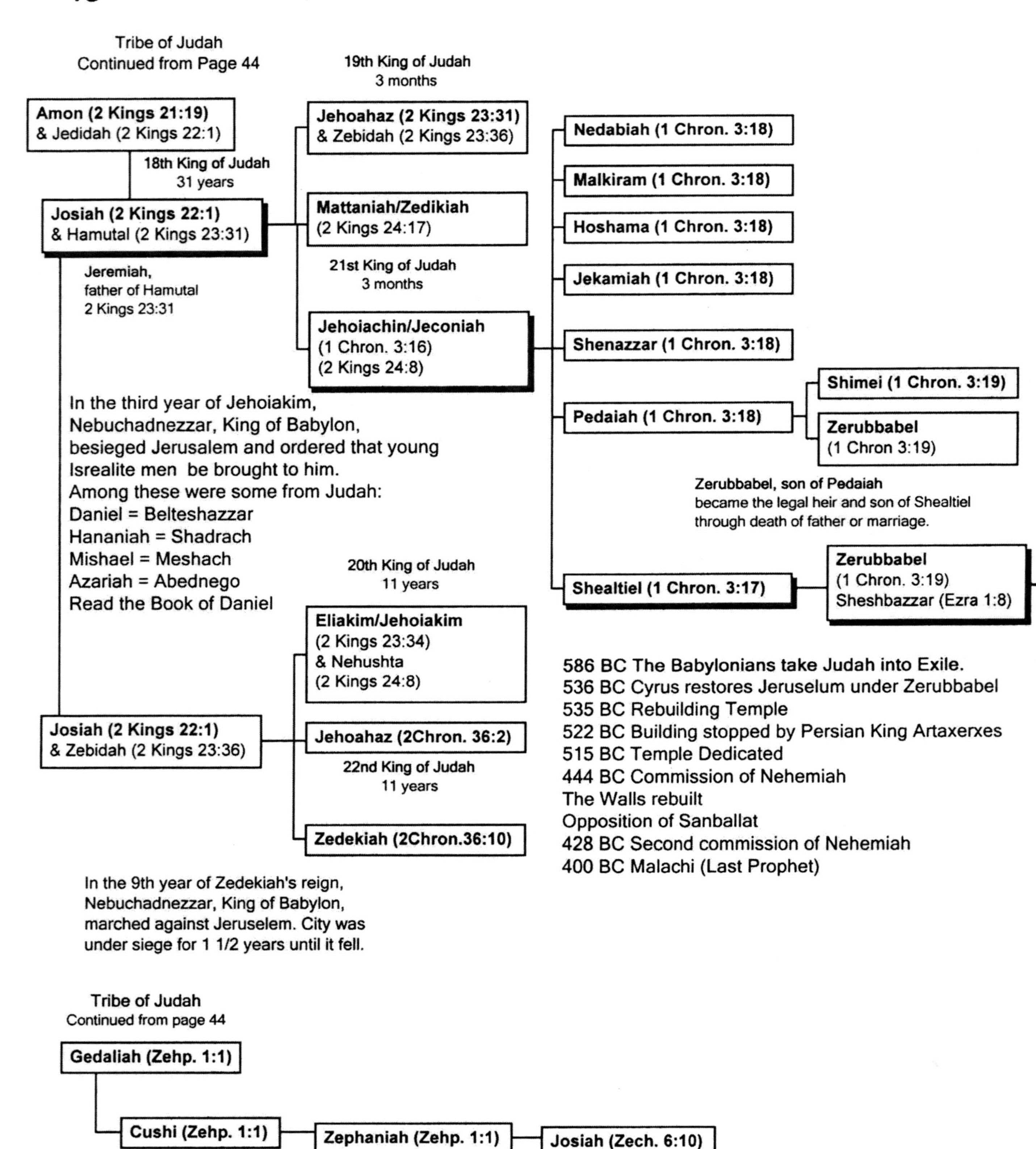
Tribe of Judah
Continued from Page 44
Amon (2 Kings 21:19)
& Jedidah (2 Kings 22:1)
18th King of Judah
31 years
Josiah (2 Kings 22:1)
& Hamutal (2 Kings 23:31)
Jeremiah,
father of Hamutal
2 Kings 23:31
19th King of Judah
3 months
Jehoahaz (2 Kings 23:31)
& Zebidah (2 Kings 23:36)
Mattaniah/Zedikiah
(2 Kings 24:17)
21st King of Judah
3 months
Jehoiachin/Jeconiah
(1 Chron. 3:16)
(2 Kings 24:8)
Nedabiah (1 Chron. 3:18)
Malkiram (1 Chron. 3:18)
Hoshama (1 Chron. 3:18)
Jekamiah (1 Chron. 3:18)
Shenazzar (1 Chron. 3:18)
Pedaiah (1 Chron. 3:18)
Shimei (1 Chron. 3:19)
Zerubbabel
(1 Chron 3:19)
Zerubbabel, son of Pedaiah
became the legal heir and son of Shealtiel
through death of father or marriage.
Shealtiel (1 Chron. 3:17)
Zerubbabel
(1 Chron. 3:19)
Sheshbazzar (Ezra 1:8)
In the third year of Jehoiakim,
Nebuchadnezzar, King of Babylon,
besieged Jerusalem and ordered that young
Isrealite men be brought to him.
Among these were some from Judah:
Daniel = Belteshazzar
Hananiah = Shadrach
Mishael = Meshach
Azariah = Abednego
Read the Book of Daniel
20th King of Judah
11 years
Eliakim/Jehoiakim
(2 Kings 23:34)
& Nehushta
(2 Kings 24:8)
Josiah (2 Kings 22:1)
& Zebidah (2 Kings 23:36)
Jehoahaz (2Chron. 36:2)
22nd King of Judah
11 years
Zedekiah (2Chron.36:10)
586 BC The Babylonians take Judah into Exile.
536 BC Cyrus restores Jeruselum under Zerubbabel
535 BC Rebuilding Temple
522 BC Building stopped by Persian King Artaxerxes
515 BC Temple Dedicated
444 BC Commission of Nehemiah
The Walls rebuilt
Opposition of Sanballat
428 BC Second commission of Nehemiah
400 BC Malachi (Last Prophet)
In the 9th year of Zedekiah's reign,
Nebuchadnezzar, King of Babylon,
marched against Jeruselem. City was
under siege for 1 1/2 years until it fell.
Tribe of Judah
Continued from page 44
Gedaliah (Zehp. 1:1)
Cushi (Zehp. 1:1)
Zephaniah (Zehp. 1:1)
Josiah (Zech. 6:10)

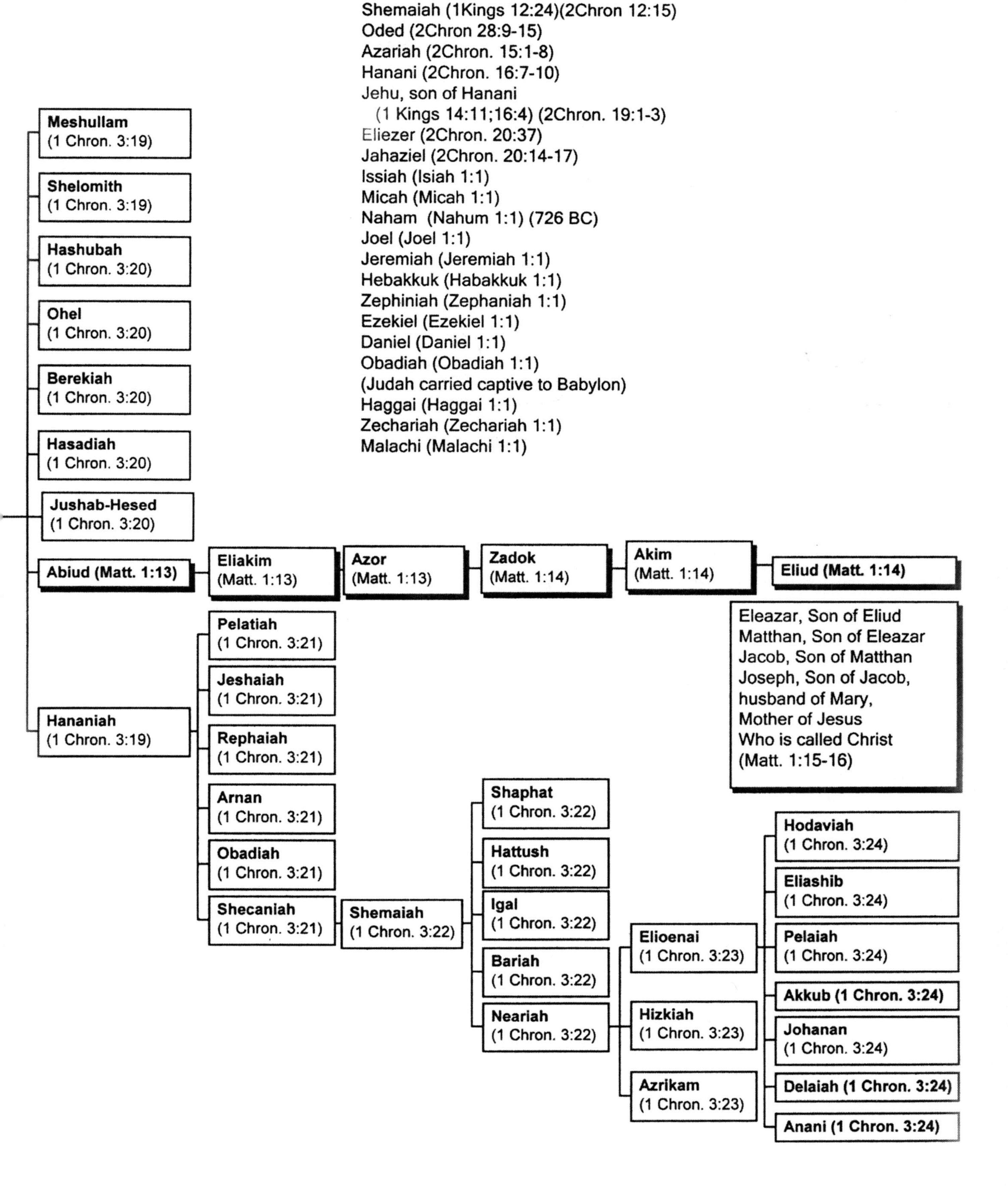
Prophets of Judah
Shemaiah (1Kings 12:24)(2Chron 12:15)
Oded (2Chron 28:9-15)
Azariah (2Chron. 15:1-8)
Hanani (2Chron. 16:7-10)
Jehu, son of Hanani
(1 Kings 14:11;16:4) (2Chron. 19:1-3)
Eliezer (2Chron. 20:37)
Jahaziel (2Chron. 20:14-17)
Issiah (Isiah 1:1)
Micah (Micah 1:1)
Naham (Nahum 1:1) (726 BC)
Joel (Joel 1:1)
Jeremiah (Jeremiah 1:1)
Hebakkuk (Habakkuk 1:1)
Zephiniah (Zephaniah 1:1)
Ezekiel (Ezekiel 1:1)
Daniel (Daniel 1:1)
Obadiah (Obadiah 1:1)
(Judah carried captive to Babylon)
Haggai (Haggai 1:1)
Zechariah (Zechariah 1:1)
Malachi (Malachi 1:1)
Meshullam (1 Chron. 3:19)
Shelomith (1 Chron. 3:19)
Hashubah (1 Chron. 3:20)
Ohel (1 Chron. 3:20)
Berekiah (1 Chron. 3:20)
Hasadiah (1 Chron. 3:20)
Jushab-Hesed (1 Chron. 3:20)
Abiud (Matt. 1:13)
Eliakim (Matt. 1:13)
Azor (Matt. 1:13)
Zadok (Matt. 1:14)
Akim (Matt. 1:14)
Eliud (Matt. 1:14)
Eleazar, Son of Eliud
Matthan, Son of Eleazar
Jacob, Son of Matthan
Joseph, Son of Jacob,
husband of Mary,
Mother of Jesus
Who is called Christ
(Matt. 1:15-16)
Hananiah (1 Chron. 3:19)
Pelatiah (1 Chron. 3:21)
Jeshaiah (1 Chron. 3:21)
Rephaiah (1 Chron. 3:21)
Arnan (1 Chron. 3:21)
Obadiah (1 Chron. 3:21)
Shecaniah (1 Chron. 3:21)
Shemaiah (1 Chron. 3:22)
Shaphat (1 Chron. 3:22)
Hattush (1 Chron. 3:22)
Igal (1 Chron. 3:22)
Bariah (1 Chron. 3:22)
Neariah (1 Chron. 3:22)
Elioenai (1 Chron. 3:23)
Hizkiah (1 Chron. 3:23)
Azrikam (1 Chron. 3:23)
Hodaviah (1 Chron. 3:24)
Eliashib (1 Chron. 3:24)
Pelaiah (1 Chron. 3:24)
Akkub (1 Chron. 3:24)
Johanan (1 Chron. 3:24)
Delaiah (1 Chron. 3:24)
Anani (1 Chron. 3:24)

Summary of the Kings
of Israel

1. Saul	reigned 42 years	Tribe of Benjamin
2. David	reigned 40 years	Tribe of Judah
3. Solomon	reigned 40 years	Tribe of Judah

(All from the Tribe Of Judah)

Kings of Judah	Reigned
4. Rehoboam	17 years
5. Abijah	3 years
6. Asa	41 years
7. Jehosphaphat	25 years
8. Jehoram	8 years
9. Ahaziah	1 year
9. Athaliah	6 years
10. Joash	40 years
11. Amaziah	29 years
12. Uzziah	52 years
13. Jotham	16 years
14. Ahaz	16 years
15. Hezekiah	29 years
16. Manasseh	55 years
17. Amon	2 years
18. Josiah	31 years
19. Jehoahaz	3 months
20. Jehoiakim	11 years
21. Jehoiachin	3months
22. Zedekiah	11 years

Kings of Israel	Reigned	Tribe
4. Jeroboam	22 years	Ephraim
5. Nadab	2 years	Ephraim
6. Baasha	24 years	Issachar
7. Elah	2 years	Issachar
8. Zimri	7 days	Benjamin
9. Tibni	see	1 Kings 16:21
9. Omri	12 years	Issachar
10. Ahab	22 years	Issachar
11. Ahaziah	2 years	Issachar
12. Joram	12 years	Issachar
13. Jehu	28 years	Gad
14. Jehoahaz	17 years	Gad
15. Jehoash	16 years	Gad
16. Jeroboam	41 years	Gad
17. Zechariah	6 months	Gad
18. Shallum	1 month	Manasseh
19. Menahem	10 years	Manasseh
20. Pekahiah	2 years	Manasseh
21. Pekah	20 years	Manasseh
22. Hoshea	9 years	Manasseh

INDEX (page#)

Aaron(27)
Abdi(33)
Abdon(18)
Abdon(19)
Abiasaph/Ebiasaph(28)
Abiathar(27)
Abiathar(28)
Abida(5)
Abiel/Jeiel(16)(19)
Abiezer(14)
Abigail(41)
Abigail(41)
Abihael(11)
Abihail(37)
Abihail(41)(42)
Abihu(27)
Abihud(46)
Abijah(11)
Abijah(14)
Abijah(15)
Abijah(34)
Abijah(35)(39)
Abijah(43)
Abimael(4)
Abimelech(14)
Abinadab(41)
Abiram(22)
Abishag(41)
Abishai(42)
Abishua(28)
Abishur(37)
Abital(41)
Abithar(27)
Abitub(17)
Abiud(46)
Able(1)
Abner(19)
Abram/Abraham(5)
Absalom(42)
Achan/Achar(35)
Acsah(36)
Acsah(39)
Adah(2)
Adah(7)(8)(22)
Adaiah(17)
Adaiah(28)
Adam(1)
Adbeel(5)
Adiel(26)
Adonijah(42)
Adriel(19)
Ahab(24)
Aharhel(40)
Ahaz(11)(44)
Ahaz(20)
Ahaziah(24)
Ahaziah(43)
Ahban(37)
Ahi(9)
Ahiezer(12)
Ahihud(16)
Ahijah(16)
Ahijah(24)
Ahijah(28)
Ahijah(30)
Ahijah(37)
Ahimaaz(29)
Ahimaaz(42)
Ahimelech(28)
Ahimelech(28)
Ahimelech(28)
Ahimoth(33)
Ahinoam(19)
Ahinoam(41)
Ahi(9)
Ahio(17)
Ahio(19)
Ahio(42)
Ahisamach(12)
Ahishahar(15)
Ahitub(28)
Ahitub(29)
Ahitub(29)
Ahlai(38)
Ahoah/Iri(15)
Ahumai(40)
Ahuzzam(39)
Aiah(8)
Akan(8)
Akim(46)
Akkub(46)
Alemeth(15)
Alemeth(21)
Allon(26)
Almodad(4)
Alvan(8)
Amal(9)
Amalak(8)
Amariah(27)
Amariah(29)
Amariah(29)
Amariah(44)
Amasa(42)
Amasai(33)
Amaziah(26)
Amaziah(28)
Amaziah(44)
Ammiel(32)
Ammihud(13)
Amminadab(41)
Ammishaddai(12)
Ammizabad(26)
Amnon(36)
Amnon(42)
Amon(44)(45)
Amoz(44)
Amram(27)
Amzi(28)
Anah(8)
Anah(8)
Anani(46)
Anathoth(15)
Anthothijah(18)
Anub(40)
Aphiah(16)
Appaim(37)(38)
Arad(17)
Arah(10)
Aram(3)
Aram(6)
Aram(9)
Aran(8)
Ara/Ulla(10)
Ardon(39)
Areli(9)
Armoni(19)
Arnan(46)
Arodi(9)
Arphaxad(3)
Asa(43)
Asahel(42)
Asaph(31)
Asarel(36)
Asarel(36)
Asenath(7)(13)
Ashbel/Jadiael(15)
Ashdenaz(3)
Asher(7)(9)
Ashhur(39)
Ashvath(9)
Asiel(26)
Asriel(13)
Asshur(3)
Assiah(26)
Assiah(28)
Assir(27)
Assir(28)
Atarah(35)(37)
Athaliah(18)
Athaliah(24)
Attai(38)
Attai(43)
Azariah(28)
Azariah(28)
Azariah(29)
Azariah(29)
Azariah(30)
Azariah(32)

Azariah(35)
Azariah(38)
Azariah(38)
Azariah(43)
Azariah/Uzziah(30)(43)
Azariahu(43)
Azel(21)
Azmaveth(21)
Azor(46)
Azrikam(21)
Azrikam(46)
Azubah(35)(39)
Azubah(43)
Baal(19)
Baara/Hodesh(16)(17)
Baaseiah(31)
Baasha(24)
Bani(28)
Bariah(46)
Basemath(5)(7)(8)(22)
Basemath(42)
Bathsheba(41)
Bathshua(7)(35)
Becorath(16)
Bedan(14)
Beeliada(42)
Beera(10)
Beker(13)
Beker/Aharah(15)
Bela(15)
Ben-Abinadab(42)
Benaiah(26)
Benaiah(26)
Ben-Ammi(6)
Ben-Hanan(36)
Benjamin(15)
Benjamin/Ben-Oni(7)(15)
Ben-Zoheth(36)
Beraiah(17)
Bered(13)
Berekiah(46)
Berekiah
Beri(10)
Beriah(9)
Beriah(13)
Beriah(17)
Beriah(27)
Beth Gader(40)
Beth Rapha(40)
Beth Zur(40)
Bethlehem(40)
Bethuel(5)
Bezalel(35)
Bezalel(40)
Bezer(10)
Bicri(18)
Bilhah(7)(12)
Bilhan(8)
Bilhan(15)
Bimhal(9)
Binea(21)
Birzaith(9)
Bithiah(36)
Boaz(41)
Bokeru(21)
Bukki(28)
Bunah(37)
Buz(5)
Buz(10)
Cain(1)
Calcol(35)
Caleb(35)(39)
Caleb(36)
Canaan(3)
Carmi(22)
Carmi(35)
Cush(3)
Cushi(45)
Dan(7)(12)
Daniel(42)
Darda(35)
Dathan(22)
David(19)(41)
Dedan(3)
Dedan(5)
Delaiah(46)
Delilah(12)
Deuel(9)
Diklah(4)
Dinah(7)
Dishan(8)
Dishon(8)
Dishon(8)
Dodo(24)
Dumah(5)
Ebal(8)
Eber(3)
Eber(11)
Eber(17)
Eber(18)
Ebiasaph(27)
Eder(17)
Eder(27)
Eglah(41)
Ehud(15)
Ehud(16)
Eker(37)
Elah(24)
Elah(36)
Elam(3)
Elam(18)
Elam(32)
Eldaah(5)
Elead(13)
Eleadah(14)
Eleasah(21)
Eleasah(38)
Eleazar(27)
Eleazar(46)
Elezer(15)
Eliab(22)
Eliab(41)
Eliab/Eliel(34)
Eliada(42)
Eliakim(46)
Eliakim/Jehoiakim(45)
Eliasaph(9)
Eliashib(46)
Eliazar/Eli(27)
Eliehoenai(32)
Eliel(17)
Eliel(18)
Elienai(17)
Eliezer(27)
Elihoreph(30)
Elijah(18)
Elioenai(15)
Elioenai(26)
Elioenai(46)
Eliphaz(7)(8)
Eliphelet(21)
Eliphelet(28)
Eliphelet(42)
Elishah(3)
Elishama(14)
Elishama(38)
Elishama(42)
Elishaphat(28)
Elisheba(27)(41)
Elishua(42)
Eliud(46)
Elkanah(28)
Elkanah(33)
Elkanah(33)
Elkanah(34)
Elon(22)
Elpaal(17)
Elpaal(17)
Elzabad(32)
Elzaphan(27)
Enoch(1)
Enoch(2)
Enosh(1)
Epah(39)
Ephah(5)
Ephah(35)(39)
Ephah(40)
Epher(5)
Epher(36)
Ephial(38)
Ephraim(07)(13)
Ephrath/Ephrathah(35)(39)
Er(35)
Er(35)
Eran(13)
Eri(9)

Esau/Edom(6)(7)(8)
Eshek(21)
Eshtemoa(36)
Eshtemoa(36)
Eshton(40)
Ethan(28)
Ethan(35)
Ethan/Jeduthun(33)
Ethnan(39)
Ethni(28)(31)
Eve(1)
Ezbon(15)
Ezbon/Ozni(9)
Ezer(8)
Ezer(13)
Ezer(39)
Ezra(30)
Ezrah(36)
Gad(7)(9)
Gaham(5)
Gatam(8)
Gazez(39)
Gazez(39)
Ge Harashim(36)
Geber(35)
Gedaliah(44)(45)
Gedor(19)
Gedor(36)
Gedor(40)
Gera(16)
Gera(16)
Gershom(27)
Gershon(27)
Geshan(40)
Gether(3)
Gibea(39)
Gideon/Jerub-Baal(14)
Gilead(11)
Gilead(13)
Gomer(3)
Guni(12)
Haahashtari(39)
Hadad(5)
Hadassah/Esther(21)
Hadoram(4)
Hagar(5)
Haggi(9)
Haggiah(28)
Haggith(41)
Ham(3)
Hameul(35)
Hammoleketh(13)
Hammuel(25)
Hamutal(45)
Hanan(21)
Hananiah(18)
Hananiah(46)
Hannah(34)
Hannan(18)
Hannani(11)
Hanniel(10)
Hanoch(5)
Hanoch(22)
Haran(5)
Haran(27)
Haran(39)
Hareph(40)
Harnepher(10)
Harum(39)
Hasadiah(46)
Hashabiah(28)(33)
Hashubah(46)
Hathath(36)
Hattush(46)
Havilah(3)
Havilah(4)
Hazarmaveth(4)
Haziel(27)
Hazo(5)
Hazzelelponi(39)
Heber(9)
Heber(17)
Heber(36)
Hebron(27)
Hebron(40)
Helah(39)
Helez(38)
Heman(34)
Heman(35)
Hepher(39)
Hephzibah(44)
Hezekiah(44)
Hezron(13)(35)
Hezron(22)
Hilkiah(28)
Hilkiah(30)
Hizki(17)
Hizkiah(46)
Hod(10)
Hodaviah(46)
Hodiah(36)
Homam(8)
Hophni(27)
Hori(8)
Hoshama(45)
Hoshea(14)
Hotham/Helem(9)
Hubbah(9)
Hul(3)
Huppites(15)
Hur(35)
Hur(39)
Huri(11)
Hushah(40)
Hushim(16)(17)
Hushim/Shuham(12)
Ibhar(42)
Ibsam(23)
Ichabod(28)
Idbash(39)
Iddo(28)
Igal(46)
Imna(9)
Imnah(9)
Imrah(10)
Iphdeiah(18)
Ir Nahash(40)
Irad(1)
Iru(36)
Isaac(5)(6)(7)
Isaiah(44)
Iscah(5)
Ishbah(36)
Ishbak(5)
Ish-Bosheth/Eshbaal(19)
Ishhod(14)
Ishi(36)
Ishi(38)
Ishma(39)
Ishmael(5)
Ishmael(21)
Ishmael(32)
Ishmerai(17)
Ishpah(17)
Ishpan(18)
Ishvah(9)
Ishvi(9)
Ishvi/Abinadab(19)
Issachar(7)(23)
Issachar(32)
Isshiah(23)
Isshiah(27)
Ithamor(27)
Ithran/Jether(10)
Ithream(42)
Izhar/Amminadab(27)
Izliah(17)
Izrahiah(23)
Jaakobah(26)
Jaareshiah(18)
Jabal(2)
Jabez/Hazzobebah(40)
Jacan(11)
Jacob(46)
Jacob/Israel(6)(7)
Jada(37)
Jahath(27)
Jahath(40)
Jahaziel(27)
Jahdai(40)
Jahdo(10)
Jahleel(22)
Jahmai(23)
Jahziel(12)
Jair(14)(35)
Jair(21)

Jakim(17)
Jakin/Jarib(25)
Jalam(7)(8)
Jamin(25)
Jamin(37)
Jamlech(26)
Janai(11)
Japheth(3)
Japhia(42)
Japhlet(9)
Jared(2)
Jarha(38)
Jashub(23)
Jathniel(32)
Javan(3)
Jeatherai(28)
Jecoliah(44)
Jedaiah(26)
Jediael(32)
Jedidah(44)(45)
Jehallelel(36)
Jehath(27)
Jehiel(27)
Jehiel(43)
Jehoaddah(20)(21)
Jehoahaz(11)
Jehoahaz(45)
Jehoash/Joash(44)
Jehohanan(32)
Jehoiachin/Jeconiah(45)
Jehoiada(26)
Jehoiada(43)
Jehoram/Joram(24)(43)
Jehoshaphat(11)
Jehoshaphat(43)
Jehosheba(43)
Jehozabad(32)
Jehozadak(30)
Jehu(11)
Jehu(26)
Jehu(38)
Jekameam(27)
Jekamiah(38)
Jekamiah(45)
Jekuthiel(36)
Jephthah(14)
Jephunneh(10)
Jephunneh(35)(36)
Jerah(4)
Jerahmeel(35)(37)
Jered(36)
Jeremiah(45)
Jeremoth(15)
Jeremoth(17)
Jeremoth(27)
Jeriah(27)
Jeriel(23)
Jerimoth(15)
Jerimoth(42)
Jeroboam(14)
Jeroboam II(11)
Jeroham(18)
Jeroham(34)
Jerusha(30)(43)
Jeshaiah(18)
Jeshaiah(28)
Jeshaiah(46)
Jesher(39)
Jeshishai(10)
Jeshohaiah(26)
Jesimiel(26)
Jesse/Nahash(41)
Jesus(46)
Jether(14)
Jether(36)
Jether(37)
Jether(41)
Jethro(27)
Jetur(5)
Jeush(7) (8)
Jeush(15)
Jeush(21)
Jeush(42)
Jeuz(17)
Jezebel(24)
Jezer(12)
Jezreel(39)
Jidlaph(5)
Jihoaddin
Joab(32)
Joab(36)
Joab(42)
Joah(28)
Joah(32)
Joash(14)
Joash(15)
Joash(35)
Jobab(4)
Jobab(17)
Jobab(17)
Jochebed(27)
Joel(11)
Joel(23)
Joel(26)
Joel(27)
Joel(28)
Joel(33)
Joel(34)
Joel(38)
Joha(17)
Johanan(29)
Johanan(46)
Johoash(11)
Jokim(35)
Jokshan(5)
Joktan(4)
Jonadab(42)
Jonathan(19)
Jonathan(27)
Jonathan(28)
Jonathan(37)
Jonathan(42)
Jorai(11)
Joram(24)
Joram(28)
Joram/Jehoram(24)(43)
Jorkeam(40)
Joroah(11)
Joseph(7)(13)
Joseph(46)
Joshibiah(26)
Joshua/Hosea(14)
Josiah(45)
Josiah(45)
Jotham(14)
Jotham(40)
Jotham(44)
Jubal(2)
Judah(7)(35)
Judith(7)(8)
Jushab-Hesed(46)
Kedar(5)
Kedemah(5)
Keilah(36)
Kelub(40)
Kemuel(5)
Kenaanah(15)
Kenan(1)
Kenaz(8)
Kenaz(36)
Kenez(36)
Kesed(5)
Keturah(5)
Kileab(42)
Kilion(41)
Kiriath Jearim(40)
Kish(19)
Kish(27)
Kish(21)
Kishi(33)
Kohath(27)
Korah(7)(8)
Korah(27)
Korah(40)
Kore(31)
Koz(39)
Laadah(35)
Laban(6)
Ladan(13)
Lahad(40)
Lamech(2)
Lamech(2)
Leah(6)(7)
Lecah(35)
Letushites(6)
Levi(7)(27)

Libni(27)
Libni/Ladan(27)
Lot(5)
Lotan(8)
Lud(3)
Maacah(5)
Maacah(13)
Maacah(35)(39)
Maacah(41)
Maacah(42)(43)
Maachah(16)(19)
Maaseiah(28)
Maaseiah(44)
Maaz(37)
Macbenah(39)
Madai(3)
Madmannah(39)
Magog(3)
Mahalalel(1)
Mahalath(5)(7)(8)
Mahalath(42)
Mahath(33)
Mahlah(14)
Mahli(27)
Mahli(27)
Mahlon(41)
Makir(13
Malcam(17)
Malkiel(9)
Malkijah(31)
Malkiram(45)
Malki-Shua(19)
Malluch(33)
Manahath(8)
Manasseh(7)(13)
Manasseh(44)
Manoah(12)
Maon(40)
Mareshah(35)
Mareshah(40)
Mary(46)
Massa(5)
Mattaniah/Zedikiah(45)
Matthan(46)
Medan(5)
Mehir(40)
Mehujael(1)
Melech(20)
Menahem(14)
Meonothai(36)
Mephibosheth(19)
Mephibosheth(20)
Merab(19)
Meraioth(28)(29)
Merari(27)
Mered(36)
Merib-Baal(20)
Mesha(17)
Mesha(39)
Meshech(3)
Meshech(3)
Meshelemiah(32)
Meshobab(26)
Meshullam(11)
Meshullam(17)
Meshullam(46)
Meshullemeth
Methuselah(2)
Methushael(2)
Mibsam(5)
Mibsam(25)
Mica(20)
Micah(5)
Micah(20)
Micah(27)
Michael(11)
Michael(11)
Michael(17)
Michael(23)
Michael(31)
Michael(43)
Michal(19)(41)
Midian(5)
Mikloth(19)
Milcah(5)
Miriam(27)
Miriam(36)
Mirmah(17)
Mishael(27)
Misham(17)
Mishma(5)
Mishma(25)
Mizraim(3)
Mizzah(6)(8)
Moab(6)
Molid(37)
Mordecai(21)
Moses(27)
Moza(21)
Moza(39)
Muppim/Shupham 21)
Mushi(27)
Naam(36)
Naamah(2)
Naamah(42)
Naaman(16)
Naarah(39)
Nebat(14)
Nadab(14)
Nadab(19)
Nadab(27)
Nadab(37)
Nahath(6)(8)
Nahath/Toah(33)
Nahor(4)
Nahor(5)
Nahshon(41)
Naomi(41)
Naphish(5)
Naphtali(7)(12)
Nathan(38)
Nathan(42)
Neariah(46)
Nebaioth(5)
Nebat(14)
Nedab(14)
Nedabiah(45)
Nehushta(45)
Nemuel(22)
Nemuel(25)
Nepheg(27)
Nepheg(42)
Ner(19)
Nethanel(32)
Nethanel(41)
Nimrod(3)
Nimshi(11)
Noah(2)
Nogah(42)
Nohah(15)
Nun(14)
Obadiah(21)
Obadiah(23)
Obadiah(46)
Obal(4)
Obed(32)
Obed(38)
Obed(41)
Obed-Edom(32)
Ohad/Zerah(25)
Ohel(46)
Oholiab(12)
Oholibamah(7)(8)
Omar(8)
Omri(15)
Omri(24)
Onam(8)
Onam(37)
Onan(35)
Ophir(4)
Ophrah(36)
Oren(37)
Orpah(41)
Othni(32)
Othniel(36)
Ozem(37)
Ozem(41)
Pallu(22)
Paltiel(19)
Pasach(9)
Paseah(40)
Pedahiah(45)
Pedaiah(14)
Pekah(14)
Pekahiah(14)
Pelaiah(46)

Pelatiah(46)
Peleg(4)
Pelet(40)
Peleth(37)
Peninnah(34)
Penuel(18)
Penuel(39)
Peresh(13)
Perez(35)
Peullethai(32)
Phinehas(27)
Pildash(5)
Pispah(10)
Pithon(20)
Puah(23)
Put(3)
Raamah(3)
Rachel(6)(7)
Raddai(41)
Rahab(41)
Raham(40)
Rakem(14)
Ram(35)(41)
Ram(37)
Rapha(15)
Raphaiah(21)
Reaiah(40)
Rebekah(5)(6)(7)
Regem(40)
Rehabiah(27)
Rehoboam(42)(43)
Rekem(40)
Rephael(32)
Rephah(13)
Rephaiah(23)
Rephaiah(36)
Rephaiah(46)
Resheph(13)
Reu(4)
Reuben(7)(22)
Reuel(6)(7)(8)
Reumah(5)
Rinnah(36)
Riphath(3)
Rizia(10)
Rizpah(19)
Rohgah(9)
Ruth(41)
Sabtah(3)
Sabtecah(3)
Sacar(32)
Sakia(17)
Salma(39)
Salmon(41)
Samson(12)
Samuel(23)
Samuel(34)
Sarai/Sarah(5)
Saraph(35)
Saul(19)
Seba(3)
Segub(14)(35)
Seled(37)
Serah(9)
Seraiah(26)
Seraiah(36)
Seraiah/Shisha(30)
Sered(22)
Serug(4)
Seth(1)
Shaaph(39)
Shaaph(40)
Shaharaim(16)(17)
Shallum(14)
Shallum(25)
Shallum(30)
Shallum(38)
Shamma(10)
Shammah(6)(8)
Shammai(36)
Shammai(37)
Shammai(40)
Shammua(42)
Shamsherai(18)
Shapham(11)
Shaphat(11)
Shaphat(46)
Shashak(17)
Shaul(25)
Shaul(28)
Shealtiel(45)
Sheariah(21)
Shear-Jashub(44)
Sheba(3)
Sheba(4)
Sheba(5)
Sheba(11)
Sheba(18)
Sheber(39)
Shecaniah(46)
Sheerah(13)
Shehariah(18)
Shelah(3)
Shelah(35)
Sheleph(4)
Shelesh(9)
Shelomith(27)
Shelomith(28)
Shelomith(43)
Shelomith(46)
Shelomoth(27)
Shem(3)
Shema(17)
Shema(40)
Shemaiah(32)
Shemaiah(46)
Shemarah(42)
Shemei(17)
Shemer(27)
Shenazzar(45)
Shephatiah(42)
Shephatiah(43)
Shepho(8)
Sheresh(13)
Shermaiah(26)
Sheshan(38)
Sheva(39)
Shilshah(10)
Shimea(28)
Shimea(31)
Shimeah/Shimea(41)
Shimeam(19)
Shimeath(14)
Shimei(21)
Shimei(25)
Shimei(27)
Shimei(27)
Shimei(27)
Shimei(28)
Shimei(45)
Shimom(36)
Shimrath(17)
Shimri(26)
Shimrith(32)
Shimron(23)
Shiphi(26)
Shobab(39)
Shobab(42)
Shobal(8)
Shobal(39)
Shomer(9)
Shua(9)
Shuah(5)
Shual(10)
Shubael(27)
Shuhah(40)
Shuni(9)
Shuppites(15)
Shuthelah(13)
Shuthelah(14)
Sidon(3)
Sillem(12)
Simeon(7)(25)
Sismai(38)
Sithri(27)
Soco(36)
Solomon/Jedidiah(42)
Sons of Seir(7)(8)
Suah(10)
Tahan(13)
Tahash(5)
Tahath(13)
Tahath(14)
Tahath(28)
Talmai(41)
Tamar(7)(35)

Tamar(42)
Tamar(42)
Taphath(42)
Tappuah(40)
Tarea(20)
Tarshish(3)
Tarshish(15)
Tebah(5)
Tehinnah(40)
Tekoa(39)
Telah(14)
Tema(5)
Teman(8)
Temeni(39)
Terah(4)
The Amorites(3)
The Anamites(3)
The Arkites(3)
The Arvadites(3)
The Asshurites(6)
The Caphtorites(3)
The Casluhites(3)
The Girgashites
The Hamathites(3)
The Hittites(3)
The Hivites(3)
The Jebusites(3)
The Kittim(3)
The Lehabites(3)
The Leummites(6)
The Ludites(3)
The Naphtuhites(3)
The Pathrusites
The Rodanim(3)
The Sinites(3)
The Zemarites(3)
Tilon(36)
Timna(7)(8)
Tiras(3)
Tirhanah(39)
Tiris(36)
Togarmah(3)
Tola(23)
Tola(24)
Tubal(3)
Tubal-Cain(2)
Ulam(14)
Ulam(21)
Uri(35)
Uri(39)
Uriel(28)
Uz(3)
Uz(5)
Uz(8)
Uzal(4)
Uzza(16)
Uzzah(28)
Uzzah(42)
Uzzi(15)
Uzzi(23)
Uzzi(28)
Uzziah(28)
Uzziel(15)
Uzziel(27)
Uzziel(36)
Zaavan(8)
Zabad(14)
Zabdi(17)
Zabud(38)
Zaccur(25)
Zadok(28)
Zadok(29)
Zadok(30)
Zadok(46)
Zaham(42)
Zanoah(36)
Zaza(37)
Zebadiah(17)
Zebadiah(17)
Zebadiah(32)
Zebidah(45)
Zebulun(7)(22)
Zechariah(11)
Zechariah(32)
Zechariah(43)
Zechariah(44)
Zedekiah(45)
Zeker(19)
Zemirah(15)
Zephaniah(28)
Zephaniah(45)
Zepho(8)
Zephon(9)
Zerah(6)(8)
Zerah(28)
Zerah(28)
Zerah(35)
Zerahiah(28)
Zereth(39)
Zeror(16)
Zeruah(14)
Zerubbabel(45)
Zerubbabel/Sheshbazzar(45)
Zeruiah(41)
Zetham(27)
Zethan(15)
Zia(11)
Zibeon(8)
Zibia(17)
Zibiah(43)
Zicri(17)
Zicri(18)
Zicri(18)
Zicri(27)
Zicri(28)
Zimmah(27)
Zimmah(28)
Zimran(5)
Zimri(21)
Zimri(35)
Ziph(36)
Ziph(39)
Ziphah(36)
Zipporah(27)
Zillah(2)
Zillethai(17)
Zilpah(7)
Ziza(26)
Ziza(27)
Ziza(43)
Zohar(25)
Zohar(39)
Zoheth(36)
Zophah(9)
Zophai/Zuph(33)
Zur(19)

Adam to Jacob

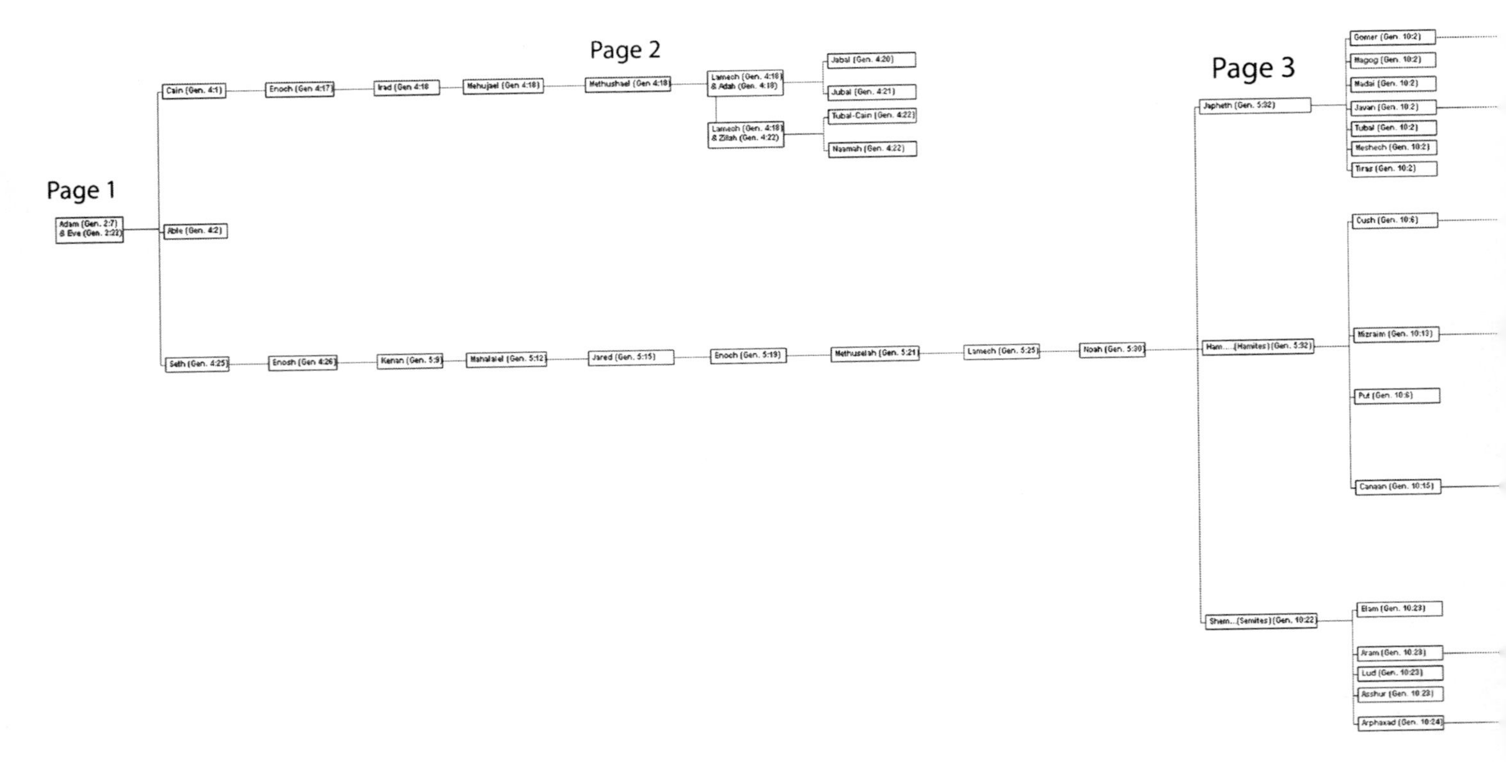

Page 1
Adam (Gen. 2:7) & Eve (Gen. 2:22)
Cain (Gen. 4:1)
Able (Gen. 4:2)
Seth (Gen. 4:25)
Enoch (Gen 4:17)
Irad (Gen 4:18
Mehujael (Gen 4:18)
Page 2
Methushael (Gen 4:18)
Lamech (Gen. 4:18) & Adah (Gen. 4:18)
Lamech (Gen. 4:18) & Zillah (Gen. 4:22)
Jabal (Gen. 4:20)
Jubal (Gen. 4:21)
Tubal-Cain (Gen. 4:22)
Naamah (Gen. 4:22)
Enosh (Gen 4:26)
Kenan (Gen. 5:9)
Mahalalel (Gen. 5:12)
Jared (Gen. 5:15)
Enoch (Gen. 5:19)
Methuselah (Gen. 5:21)
Lamech (Gen. 5:25)
Noah (Gen. 5:30)
Page 3
Japheth (Gen. 5:32)
Ham.....(Hamites) (Gen. 5:32)
Shem...(Semites) (Gen. 10:22)
Gomer (Gen. 10:2)
Magog (Gen. 10:2)
Madai (Gen. 10:2)
Javan (Gen. 10:2)
Tubal (Gen. 10:2)
Meshech (Gen. 10:2)
Tiras (Gen. 10:2)
Cush (Gen. 10:6)
Mizraim (Gen. 10:13)
Put (Gen. 10:6)
Canaan (Gen. 10:15)
Elam (Gen. 10:23)
Aram (Gen. 10:23)
Lud (Gen. 10:23)
Asshur (Gen. 10:23)
Arphaxad (Gen. 10:24)

Generation

1 2 3 4 5 6 7 8 9 10 11 12

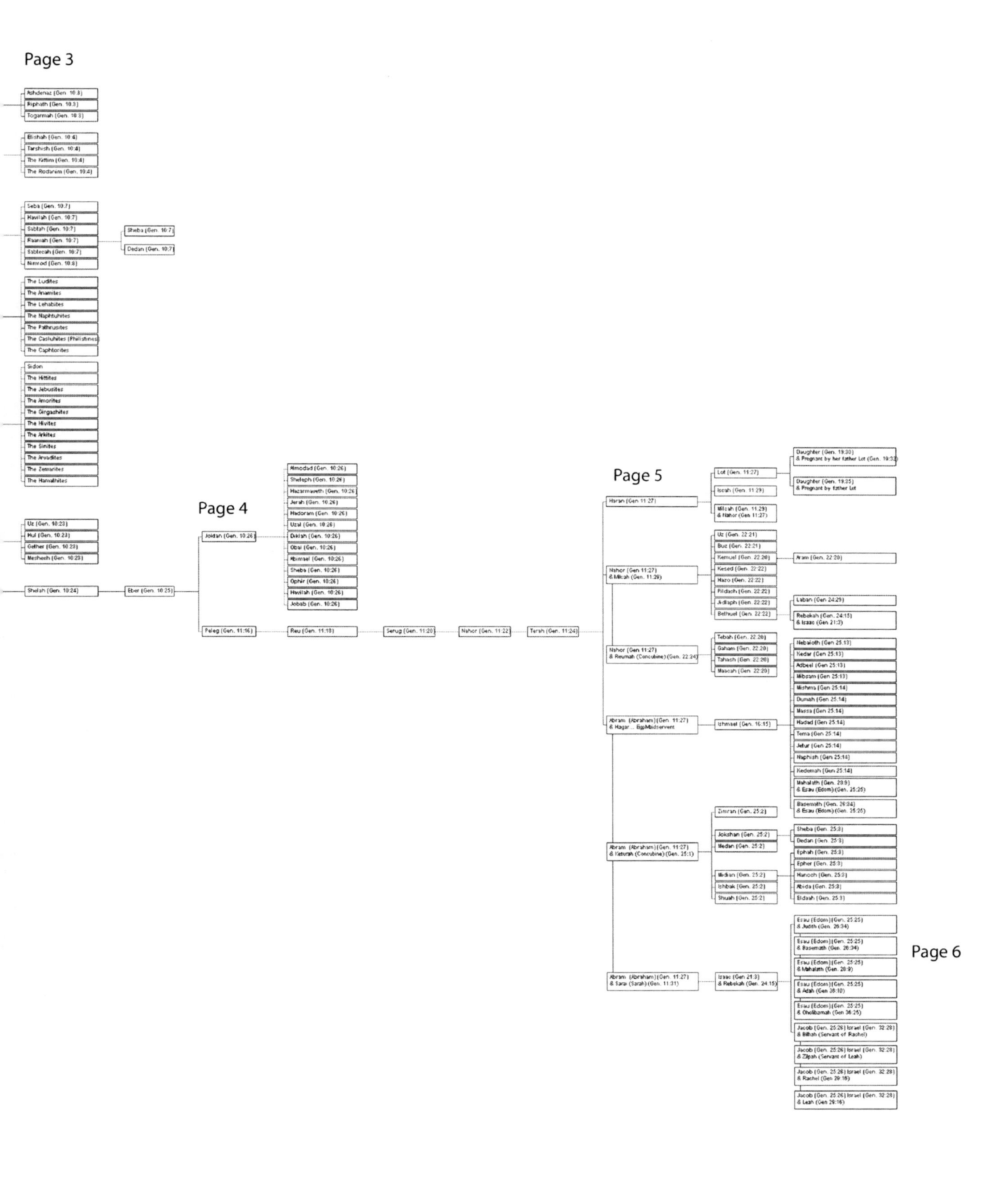
Page 3
Ashdenaz (Gen. 10:3)
Riphath (Gen. 10:3)
Togarmah (Gen. 10:3)
Elishah (Gen. 10:4)
Tarshish (Gen. 10:4)
The Kittim (Gen. 10:4)
The Rodanim (Gen. 10:4)
Seba (Gen. 10:7)
Havilah (Gen. 10:7)
Sabtah (Gen. 10:7)
Raamah (Gen. 10:7)
Sabtecah (Gen. 10:7)
Nimrod (Gen. 10:8)
Sheba (Gen. 10:7)
Dedan (Gen. 10:7)
The Ludites
The Anamites
The Lehabites
The Naphtuhites
The Pathrusites
The Casluhites (Philistines)
The Caphtorites
Sidon
The Hittites
The Jebusites
The Amorites
The Girgashites
The Hivites
The Arkites
The Sinites
The Arvadites
The Zemarites
The Hamathites
Uz (Gen. 10:23)
Hul (Gen. 10:23)
Gether (Gen. 10:23)
Mesheoh (Gen. 10:23)
Shelah (Gen. 10:24)
Eber (Gen. 10:25)
Page 4
Joktan (Gen. 10:26)
Almodad (Gen. 10:26)
Sheleph (Gen. 10:26)
Hazarmaveth (Gen. 10:26)
Jerah (Gen. 10:26)
Hadoram (Gen. 10:26)
Uzal (Gen. 10:26)
Diklah (Gen. 10:26)
Obal (Gen. 10:26)
Abimael (Gen. 10:26)
Sheba (Gen. 10:26)
Ophir (Gen. 10:26)
Havilah (Gen. 10:26)
Jobab (Gen. 10:26)
Peleg (Gen. 11:16)
Reu (Gen. 11:18)
Serug (Gen. 11:20)
Nahor (Gen. 11:22)
Terah (Gen. 11:24)
Page 5
Haran (Gen 11:27)
Lot (Gen. 11:27)
Iscah (Gen. 11:29)
Milcah (Gen. 11:29)
& Nahor (Gen 11:27)
Daughter (Gen. 19:30)
& Pregnant by her father Lot (Gen. 19:33)
Daughter (Gen. 19:35)
& Pregnant by father Lot
Nahor (Gen 11:27)
& Milcah (Gen. 11:29)
Uz (Gen. 22:21)
Buz (Gen. 22:21)
Kemuel (Gen. 22:20)
Kesed (Gen. 22:22)
Hazo (Gen. 22:22)
Pildash (Gen. 22:22)
Jidlaph (Gen. 22:22)
Bethuel (Gen. 22:22)
Aram (Gen. 22:20)
Laban (Gen 24:29)
Rebekah (Gen. 24:15)
& Isaac (Gen 21:3)
Nahor (Gen 11:27)
& Reumah (Concubine) (Gen. 22:24)
Tebah (Gen. 22:20)
Gaham (Gen. 22:20)
Tahash (Gen. 22:20)
Maacah (Gen. 22:20)
Abram (Abraham) (Gen. 11:27)
& Hagar... EgpMaidservent
Ishmael (Gen. 16:15)
Nebaioth (Gen 25:13)
Kedar (Gen 25:13)
Adbeel (Gen 25:13)
Mibsam (Gen 25:13)
Mishma (Gen 25:14)
Dumah (Gen 25:14)
Massa (Gen 25:14)
Hadad (Gen 25:14)
Tema (Gen 25:14)
Jetur (Gen 25:14)
Naphish (Gen 25:14)
Kedemah (Gen 25:14)
Mahalath (Gen. 28:9)
& Esau (Edom) (Gen. 25:25)
Basemath (Gen. 26:34)
& Esau (Edom) (Gen. 25:25)
Abram (Abraham) (Gen. 11:27)
& Keturah (Concubine) (Gen. 25:1)
Zimran (Gen. 25:2)
Jokshan (Gen. 25:2)
Medan (Gen. 25:2)
Midian (Gen. 25:2)
Ishbak (Gen. 25:2)
Shuah (Gen. 25:2)
Sheba (Gen. 25:3)
Dedan (Gen. 25:3)
Ephah (Gen. 25:3)
Epher (Gen. 25:3)
Hanoch (Gen. 25:3)
Abida (Gen. 25:3)
Eldaah (Gen. 25:3)
Abram (Abraham) (Gen. 11:27)
& Sarai (Sarah) (Gen. 11:31)
Isaac (Gen 21:3)
& Rebekah (Gen. 24:15)
Esau (Edom) (Gen. 25:25)
& Judith (Gen. 26:34)
Esau (Edom) (Gen. 25:25)
& Basemath (Gen. 26:34)
Esau (Edom) (Gen. 25:25)
& Mahalath (Gen. 28:9)
Esau (Edom) (Gen. 25:25)
& Adah (Gen 36:10)
Esau (Edom) (Gen. 25:25)
& Oholibamah (Gen 36:25)
Jacob (Gen. 25:26) Israel (Gen. 32:28)
& Bilhah (Servant of Rachel)
Jacob (Gen. 25:26) Israel (Gen. 32:28)
& Zilpah (Servant of Leah)
Jacob (Gen. 25:26) Israel (Gen. 32:28)
& Rachel (Gen 29:16)
Jacob (Gen. 25:26) Israel (Gen. 32:28)
& Leah (Gen 29:16)
Page 6
13 14 15 16 17 18 19 20 21 22

Tribe of Benjamin

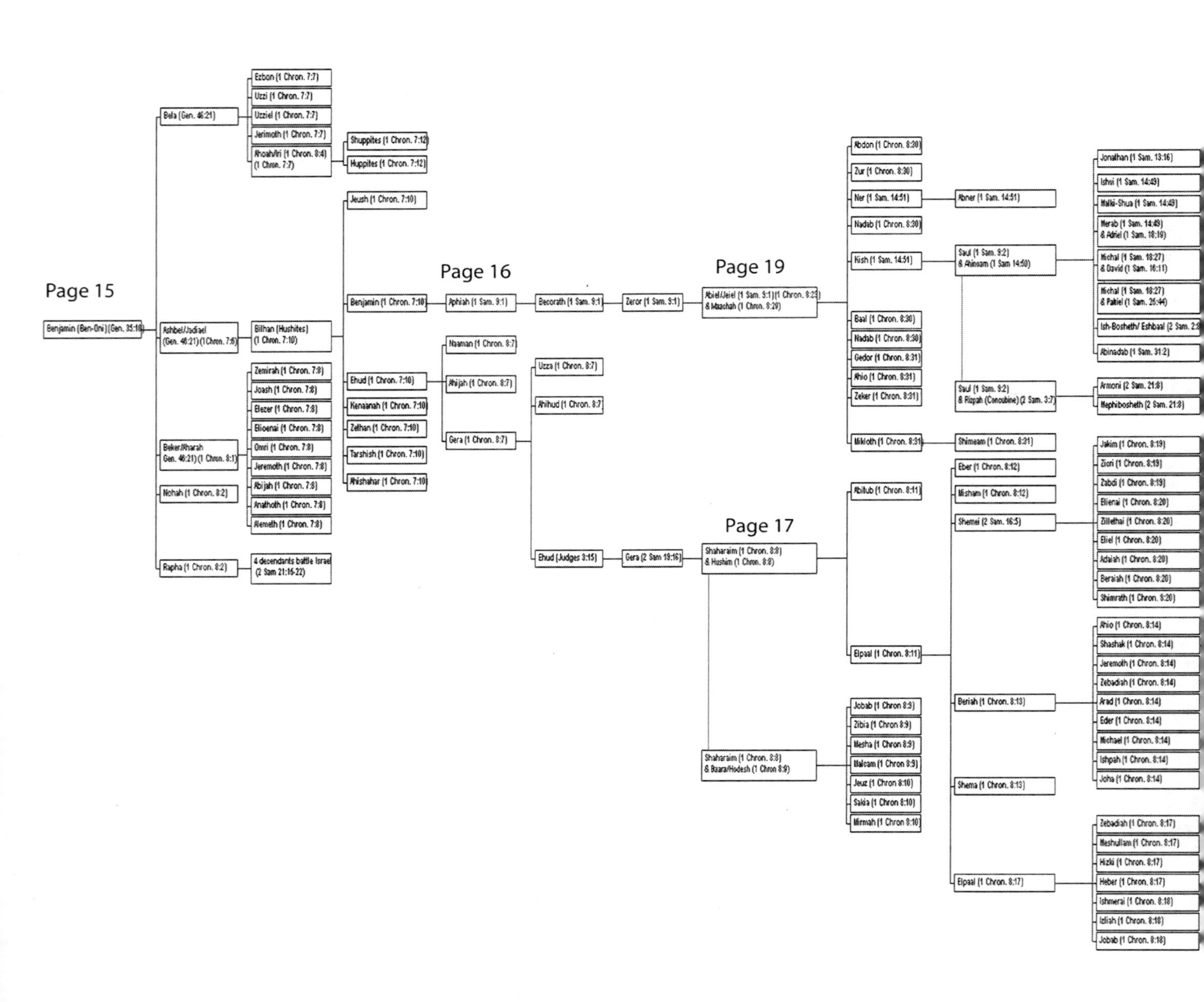
Page 15
Benjamin (Ben-Oni) (Gen. 35:18)
Bela (Gen. 46:21)
Ezbon (1 Chron. 7:7)
Uzzi (1 Chron. 7:7)
Uzziel (1 Chron. 7:7)
Jerimoth (1 Chron. 7:7)
Ahoah/Iri (1 Chron. 8:4) (1 Chron. 7:7)
Shuppites (1 Chron. 7:12)
Huppites (1 Chron. 7:12)
Ashbel/Jadiael (Gen. 46:21) (1 Chron. 7:6)
Bilhan (Hushites) (1 Chron. 7:10)
Jeush (1 Chron. 7:10)
Benjamin (1 Chron. 7:10)
Ehud (1 Chron. 7:10)
Kenaanah (1 Chron. 7:10)
Zethan (1 Chron. 7:10)
Tarshish (1 Chron. 7:10)
Ahishahar (1 Chron. 7:10)
Beker/Aharah Gen. 46:21) (1 Chron. 8:1)
Zemirah (1 Chron. 7:8)
Joash (1 Chron. 7:8)
Elezer (1 Chron. 7:8)
Elioenai (1 Chron. 7:8)
Omri (1 Chron. 7:8)
Jeremoth (1 Chron. 7:8)
Abijah (1 Chron. 7:8)
Anathoth (1 Chron. 7:8)
Alemeth (1 Chron. 7:8)
Nohah (1 Chron. 8:2)
Rapha (1 Chron. 8:2)
4 decendants battle Israel (2 Sam 21:16-22)
Page 16
Aphiah (1 Sam. 9:1)
Becorath (1 Sam. 9:1)
Zeror (1 Sam. 9:1)
Naaman (1 Chron. 8:7)
Ahijah (1 Chron. 8:7)
Gera (1 Chron. 8:7)
Uzza (1 Chron. 8:7)
Ahihud (1 Chron. 8:7
Ehud (Judges 3:15)
Gera (2 Sam 19:16)
Page 19
Abiel/Jeiel (1 Sam. 9:1) (1 Chron. 8:29) & Maachah (1 Chron. 8:29)
Abdon (1 Chron. 8:30)
Zur (1 Chron. 8:30)
Ner (1 Sam. 14:51)
Nadab (1 Chron. 8:30)
Kish (1 Sam. 14:51)
Baal (1 Chron. 8:30)
Nadab (1 Chron. 8:30)
Gedor (1 Chron. 8:31)
Ahio (1 Chron. 8:31)
Zeker (1 Chron. 8:31)
Mikloth (1 Chron. 8:31)
Abner (1 Sam. 14:51)
Saul (1 Sam. 9:2) & Ahinoam (1 Sam 14:50)
Saul (1 Sam. 9:2) & Rizpah (Concubine) (2 Sam. 3:7)
Shimeam (1 Chron. 8:31)
Jonathan (1 Sam. 13:16)
Ishvi (1 Sam. 14:49)
Malki-Shua (1 Sam. 14:49)
Merab (1 Sam. 14:49) & Adriel (1 Sam. 18:19)
Michal (1 Sam. 18:27) & David (1 Sam. 16:11)
Michal (1 Sam. 18:27) & Paltiel (1 Sam. 25:44)
Ish-Bosheth/ Eshbaal (2 Sam. 2:8
Abinadab (1 Sam. 31:2)
Armoni (2 Sam. 21:8)
Mephibosheth (2 Sam. 21:8)
Page 17
Shaharaim (1 Chron. 8:8) & Hushim (1 Chron. 8:8)
Abitub (1 Chron. 8:11)
Elpaal (1 Chron. 8:11)
Shaharaim (1 Chron. 8:8) & Baara/Hodesh (1 Chron 8:9)
Jobab (1 Chron 8:9)
Zibia (1 Chron 8:9)
Mesha (1 Chron 8:9)
Malcam (1 Chron 8:9)
Jeuz (1 Chron 8:10)
Sakia (1 Chron 8:10)
Mirmah (1 Chron 8:10)
Eber (1 Chron. 8:12)
Misham (1 Chron. 8:12)
Shemei (2 Sam. 16:5)
Beriah (1 Chron. 8:13)
Shema (1 Chron. 8:13)
Elpaal (1 Chron. 8:17)
Jakim (1 Chron. 8:19)
Zicri (1 Chron. 8:19)
Zabdi (1 Chron. 8:19)
Elienai (1 Chron. 8:20)
Zillethai (1 Chron. 8:20)
Eliel (1 Chron. 8:20)
Adaiah (1 Chron. 8:20)
Beraiah (1 Chron. 8:20)
Shimrath (1 Chron. 8:20)
Ahio (1 Chron. 8:14)
Shashak (1 Chron. 8:14)
Jeremoth (1 Chron. 8:14)
Zebadiah (1 Chron. 8:14)
Arad (1 Chron. 8:14)
Eder (1 Chron. 8:14)
Michael (1 Chron. 8:14)
Ishpah (1 Chron. 8:14)
Joha (1 Chron. 8:14)
Zebadiah (1 Chron. 8:17)
Meshullam (1 Chron. 8:17)
Hizki (1 Chron. 8:17)
Heber (1 Chron. 8:17)
Ishmerai (1 Chron. 8:18)
Izliah (1 Chron. 8:18)
Jobab (1 Chron. 8:18)

Generation from
Adam

23 24 25 26 27 28 29 30 31 32 33

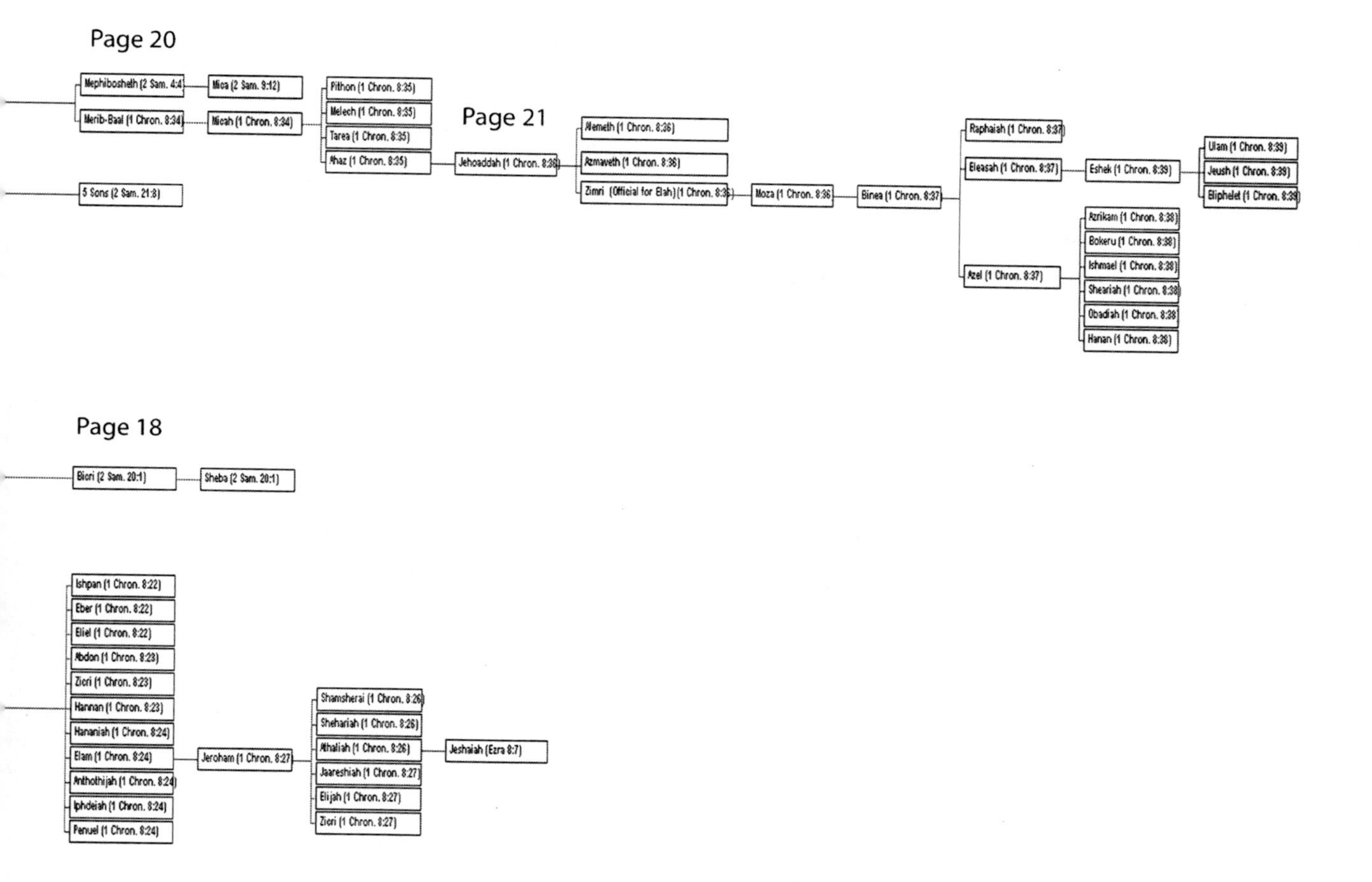
Page 20
Mephibosheth (2 Sam. 4:4)
Mica (2 Sam. 9:12)
Merib-Baal (1 Chron. 8:34)
Micah (1 Chron. 8:34)
Pithon (1 Chron. 8:35)
Melech (1 Chron. 8:35)
Tarea (1 Chron. 8:35)
Ahaz (1 Chron. 8:35)
Page 21
Jehoaddah (1 Chron. 8:36)
Alemeth (1 Chron. 8:36)
Azmaveth (1 Chron. 8:36)
Zimri (Official for Elah) (1 Chron. 8:36)
Moza (1 Chron. 8:36
Binea (1 Chron. 8:37)
Raphaiah (1 Chron. 8:37)
Eleasah (1 Chron. 8:37)
Eshek (1 Chron. 8:39)
Ulam (1 Chron. 8:39)
Jeush (1 Chron. 8:39)
Eliphelet (1 Chron. 8:39)
Azel (1 Chron. 8:37)
Azrikam (1 Chron. 8:38)
Bokeru (1 Chron. 8:38)
Ishmael (1 Chron. 8:38)
Sheariah (1 Chron. 8:38)
Obadiah (1 Chron. 8:38)
Hanan (1 Chron. 8:38)
5 Sons (2 Sam. 21:8)
Page 18
Bicri (2 Sam. 20:1)
Sheba (2 Sam. 20:1)
Ishpan (1 Chron. 8:22)
Eber (1 Chron. 8:22)
Eliel (1 Chron. 8:22)
Abdon (1 Chron. 8:23)
Zicri (1 Chron. 8:23)
Hannan (1 Chron. 8:23)
Hananiah (1 Chron. 8:24)
Elam (1 Chron. 8:24)
Anthothijah (1 Chron. 8:24)
Iphdeiah (1 Chron. 8:24)
Penuel (1 Chron. 8:24)
Jeroham (1 Chron. 8:27)
Shamsherai (1 Chron. 8:26)
Shehariah (1 Chron. 8:26)
Athaliah (1 Chron. 8:26)
Jaareshiah (1 Chron. 8:27)
Elijah (1 Chron. 8:27)
Zicri (1 Chron. 8:27)
Jeshaiah (Ezra 8:7)

34 35 36 37 38 39 40 41 42 43

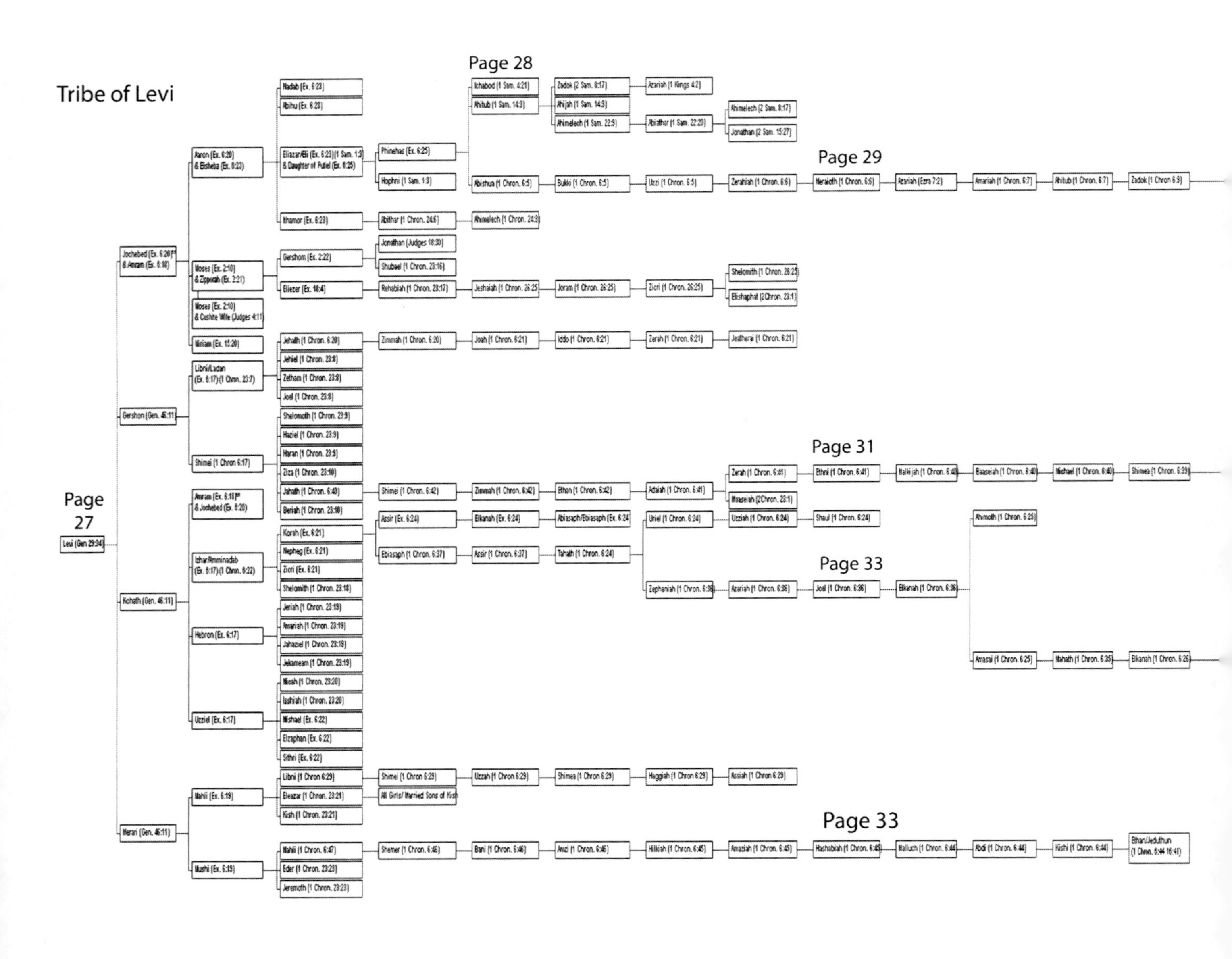
Tribe of Levi
Page 28
Nadab (Ex. 6:23)
Abihu (Ex. 6:23)
Ichabod (1 Sam. 4:21)
Ahitub (1 Sam. 14:3)
Zadok (2 Sam. 8:17)
Azariah (1 Kings 4:2)
Ahijah (1 Sam. 14:3)
Ahimelech (1 Sam. 22:9)
Abiathar (1 Sam. 22:20)
Ahimelech (2 Sam. 8:17)
Jonathan (2 Sam. 15:27)
Aaron (Ex. 6:20)
& Elisheba (Ex. 6:23)
Eliazar/Eli (Ex. 6:23)(1 Sam. 1:3)
& Daughter of Putiel (Ex. 6:25)
Phinehas (Ex. 6:25)
Hophni (1 Sam. 1:3)
Page 29
Abishua (1 Chron. 6:5)
Bukki (1 Chron. 6:5)
Uzzi (1 Chron. 6:5)
Zerahiah (1 Chron. 6:6)
Meraioth (1 Chron. 6:6)
Azariah (Ezra 7:2)
Amariah (1 Chron. 6:7)
Ahitub (1 Chron. 6:7)
Zadok (1 Chron 6:9)
Ithamor (Ex. 6:23)
Abithar (1 Chron. 24:6)
Ahimelech (1 Chron. 24:3)
Jochebed (Ex. 6:20)**
& Amram (Ex. 6:18)
Jonathan (Judges 18:30)
Gershom (Ex. 2:22)
Shubael (1 Chron. 23:16)
Moses (Ex. 2:10)
& Zipporah (Ex. 2:21)
Eliezer (Ex. 18:4)
Rehabiah (1 Chron. 23:17)
Jeshaiah (1 Chron. 26:25)
Joram (1 Chron. 26:25)
Zicri (1 Chron. 26:25)
Shelomith (1 Chron. 26:25)
Elishaphat (2Chron. 23:1)
Moses (Ex. 2:10)
& Cushite Wife (Judges 4:11)
Miriam (Ex. 15:20)
Jehath (1 Chron. 6:20)
Zimmah (1 Chron. 6:20)
Joah (1 Chron. 6:21)
Iddo (1 Chron. 6:21)
Zerah (1 Chron. 6:21)
Jeatherai (1 Chron. 6:21)
Libni/Ladan
(Ex. 6:17)(1 Chron. 23:7)
Jehiel (1 Chron. 23:8)
Zetham (1 Chron. 23:8)
Joel (1 Chron. 23:8)
Gershon (Gen. 46:11)
Shelomoth (1 Chron. 23:9)
Haziel (1 Chron. 23:9)
Haran (1 Chron. 23:9)
Page 31
Shimei (1 Chron 6:17)
Ziza (1 Chron. 23:10)
Zerah (1 Chron. 6:41)
Ethni (1 Chron. 6:41)
Malkijah (1 Chron. 6:40)
Baaseiah (1 Chron. 6:40)
Michael (1 Chron. 6:40)
Shimea (1 Chron. 6:39)
Page
27
Amram (Ex. 6:18)**
& Jochebed (Ex. 6:20)
Jahath (1 Chron. 6:43)
Shimei (1 Chron. 6:42)
Zimmah (1 Chron. 6:42)
Ethan (1 Chron. 6:42)
Adaiah (1 Chron. 6:41)
Maaseiah (2Chron. 23:1)
Beriah (1 Chron. 23:10)
Assir (Ex. 6:24)
Elkanah (Ex. 6:24)
Abiasaph/Ebiasaph (Ex. 6:24)
Uriel (1 Chron. 6:24)
Uzziah (1 Chron. 6:24)
Shaul (1 Chron. 6:24)
Ahimoth (1 Chron. 6:25)
Levi (Gen 29:34)
Korah (Ex. 6:21)
Nepheg (Ex. 6:21)
Ebiasaph (1 Chron. 6:37)
Assir (1 Chron. 6:37)
Tahath (1 Chron. 6:24)
Izhar/Amminadab
(Ex. 6:17)(1 Chron. 6:22)
Zicri (Ex. 6:21)
Page 33
Shelomith (1 Chron. 23:18)
Zephaniah (1 Chron. 6:36)
Azariah (1 Chron. 6:36)
Joel (1 Chron. 6:36)
Elkanah (1 Chron. 6:36)
Kohath (Gen. 46:11)
Jeriah (1 Chron. 23:19)
Amariah (1 Chron. 23:19)
Hebron (Ex. 6:17)
Jahaziel (1 Chron. 23:19)
Jekameam (1 Chron. 23:19)
Amasai (1 Chron. 6:25)
Mahath (1 Chron. 6:35)
Elkanah (1 Chron. 6:26)
Micah (1 Chron. 23:20)
Isshiah (1 Chron. 23:20)
Uzziel (Ex. 6:17)
Mishael (Ex. 6:22)
Elzaphan (Ex. 6:22)
Sithri (Ex. 6:22)
Libni (1 Chron 6:29)
Shimei (1 Chron 6:29)
Uzzah (1 Chron 6:29)
Shimea (1 Chron 6:29)
Haggiah (1 Chron 6:29)
Assiah (1 Chron 6:29)
Mahli (Ex. 6:19)
Eleazar (1 Chron. 23:21)
All Girls/ Married Sons of Kish
Kish (1 Chron. 23:21)
Page 33
Merari (Gen. 46:11)
Mahli (1 Chron. 6:47)
Shemer (1 Chron. 6:46)
Bani (1 Chron. 6:46)
Amzi (1 Chron. 6:46)
Hilkiah (1 Chron. 6:45)
Amaziah (1 Chron. 6:45)
Hashabiah (1 Chron. 6:45)
Malluch (1 Chron. 6:44)
Abdi (1 Chron. 6:44)
Kishi (1 Chron. 6:44)
Ethan/Jeduthun
(1 Chron. 6:44 16:41)
Mushi (Ex. 6:19)
Eder (1 Chron. 23:23)
Jeremoth (1 Chron. 23:23)

Generation from Adam

23 24 25 26 27 28 29 30 31 32 33 34 35 36

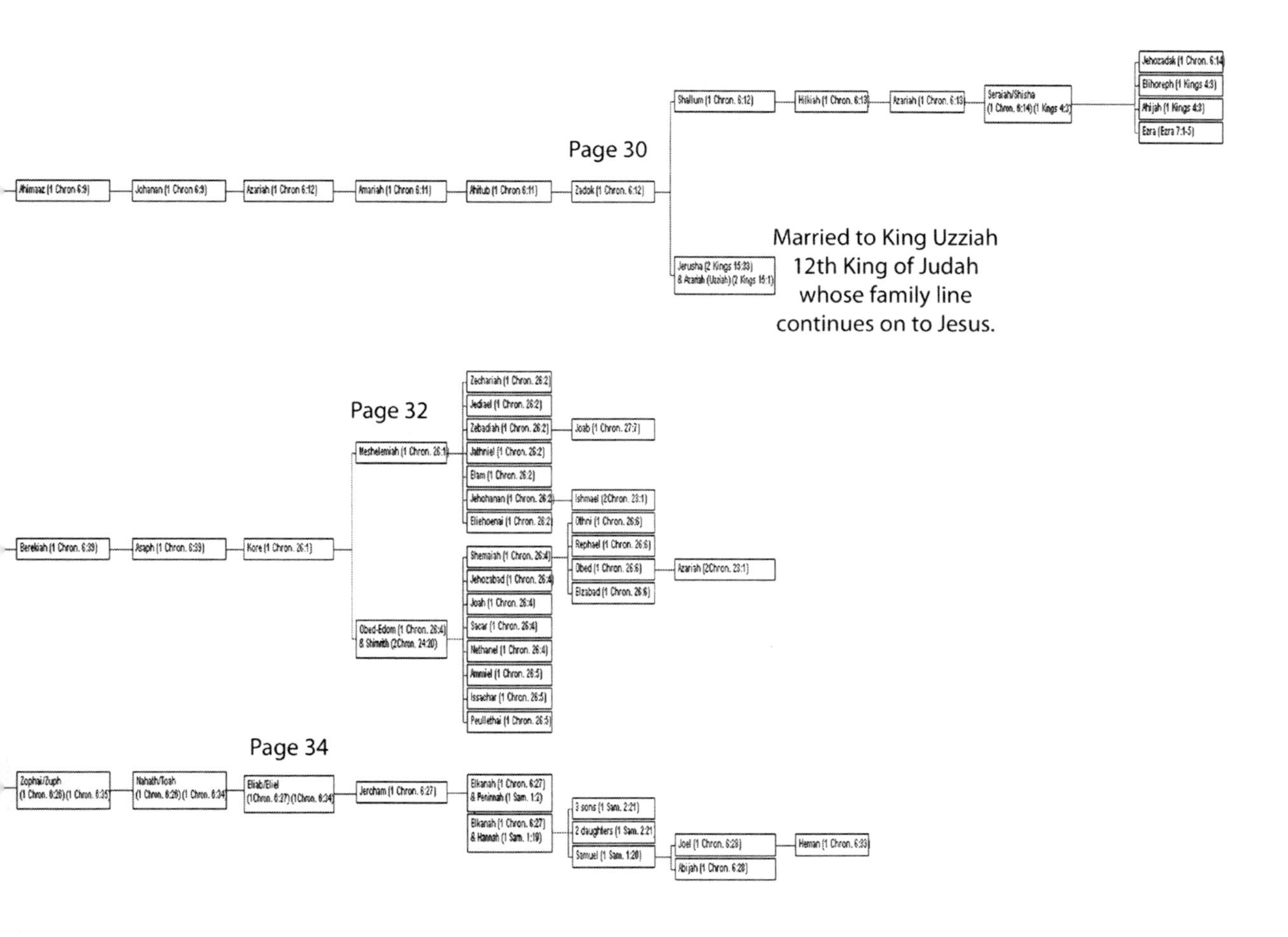
Page 30
Ahimaaz (1 Chron 6:9)
Johanan (1 Chron 6:9)
Azariah (1 Chron 6:12)
Amariah (1 Chron 6:11)
Ahitub (1 Chron 6:11)
Zadok (1 Chron. 6:12)
Shallum (1 Chron. 6:12)
Hilkiah (1 Chron. 6:13)
Azariah (1 Chron. 6:13)
Seraiah/Shisha (1 Chron. 6:14) (1 Kings 4:3)
Jehozadak (1 Chron. 6:14)
Elihoreph (1 Kings 4:3)
Ahijah (1 Kings 4:3)
Ezra (Ezra 7:1-5)
Jerusha (2 Kings 15:33) & Azariah (Uzziah) (2 Kings 15:1)
Married to King Uzziah
12th King of Judah
whose family line
continues on to Jesus.
Page 32
Berekiah (1 Chron. 6:39)
Asaph (1 Chron. 6:39)
Kore (1 Chron. 26:1)
Meshelemiah (1 Chron. 26:1)
Zechariah (1 Chron. 26:2)
Jediael (1 Chron. 26:2)
Zebadiah (1 Chron. 26:2)
Joab (1 Chron. 27:7)
Jathniel (1 Chron. 26:2)
Elam (1 Chron. 26:2)
Jehohanan (1 Chron. 26:2)
Ishmael (2Chron. 23:1)
Eliehoenai (1 Chron. 26:2)
Obed-Edom (1 Chron. 26:4) & Shimrith (2Chron. 24:20)
Shemaiah (1 Chron. 26:4)
Othni (1 Chron. 26:6)
Rephael (1 Chron. 26:6)
Obed (1 Chron. 26:6)
Azariah (2Chron. 23:1)
Elzabad (1 Chron. 26:6)
Jehozabad (1 Chron. 26:4)
Joah (1 Chron. 26:4)
Sacar (1 Chron. 26:4)
Nethanel (1 Chron. 26:4)
Ammiel (1 Chron. 26:5)
Issachar (1 Chron. 26:5)
Peullethai (1 Chron. 26:5)
Page 34
Zophai/Zuph (1 Chron. 6:26) (1 Chron. 6:35)
Nahath/Toah (1 Chron. 6:26) (1 Chron. 6:34)
Eliab/Eliel (1Chron. 6:27) (1Chron. 6:34)
Jercham (1 Chron. 6:27)
Elkanah (1 Chron. 6:27) & Peninnah (1 Sam. 1:2)
Elkanah (1 Chron. 6:27) & Hannah (1 Sam. 1:19)
3 sons (1 Sam. 2:21)
2 daughters (1 Sam. 2:21)
Samuel (1 Sam. 1:20)
Joel (1 Chron. 6:28)
Heman (1 Chron. 6:33)
Abijah (1 Chron. 6:28)

37 38 39 40 41 42 43 44 45 46 47

Tribe of Judah/Tamar

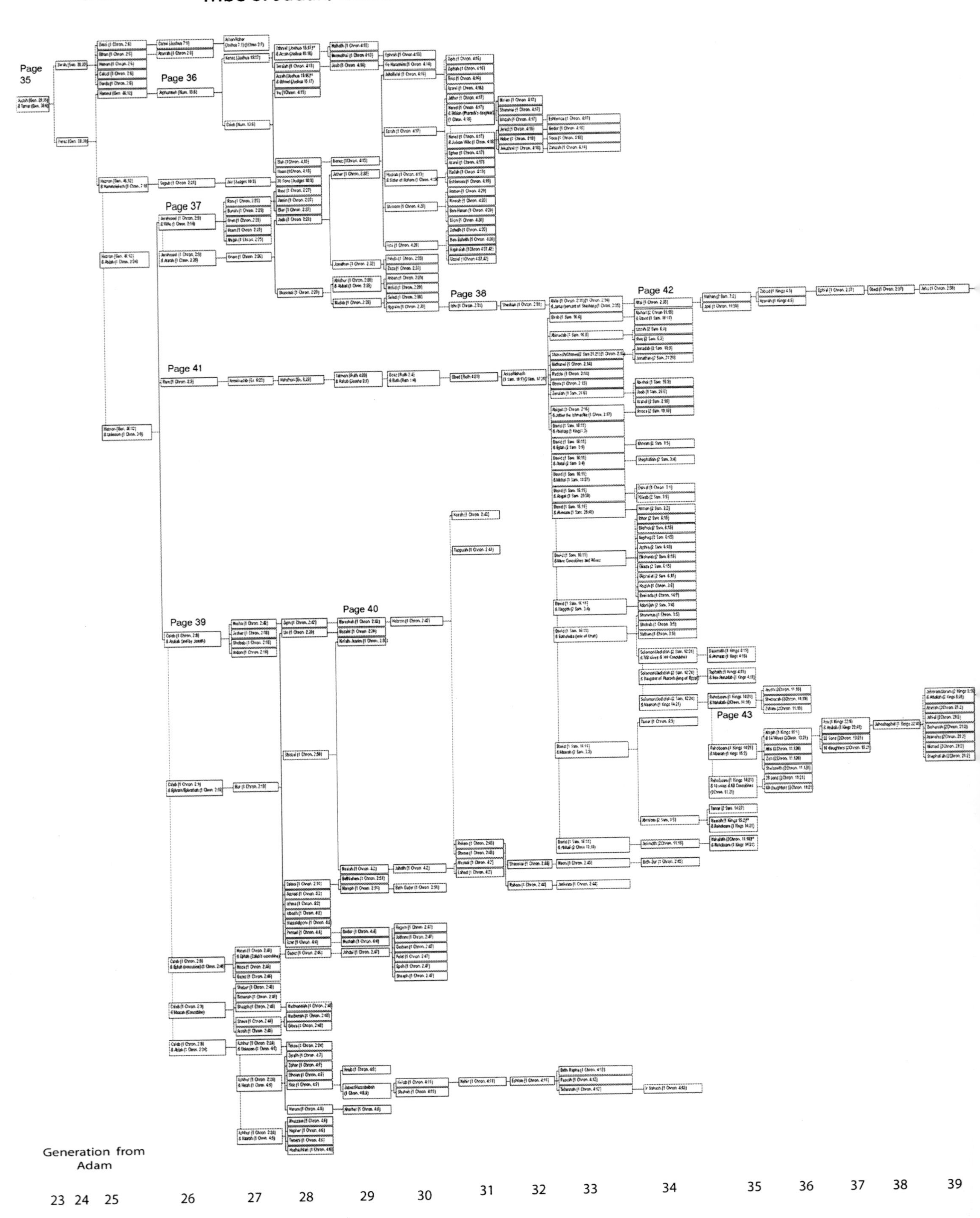

Page 35
Page 36
Page 37
Page 38
Page 39
Page 40
Page 41
Page 42
Page 43
Generation from Adam
23 24 25 26 27 28 29 30 31 32 33 34 35 36 37 38 39

Page 38

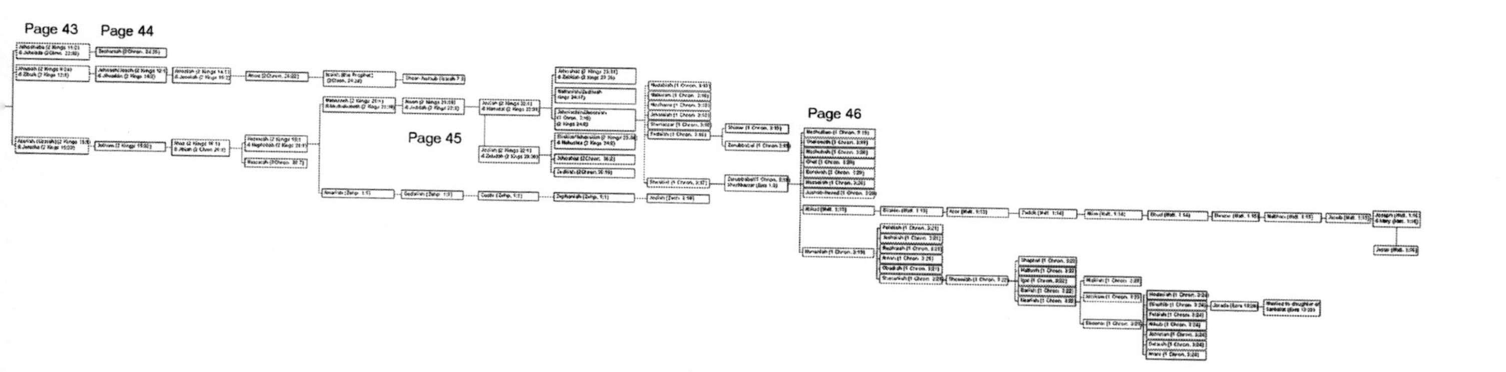
Page 43
Page 44
Page 45
Page 46

40 41 42 43 44 45 46 47 48 49 50 51 52 53 54 55 56 57 5 8 59

60

Resources

The Holy Bible, New International Version, Zondervan Bible Publishers, Grand Rapids, Michigan, 1978

Compton's Interactive Bible, CD Rom, Version 1.0, New International Version, Zondervan Publishing House, 1996

Generations 4.2 and 6.0, Deluxe Edition, Family Tree Software, Sierra Home, 1998

Breinigsville, PA USA
07 December 2009
228783BV00003B/1/P
9 781934 749326